The Interfact

New Metaphysics

Series Editors: Graham Harman and Bruno Latour

The world is due for a resurgence of original speculative metaphysics. The New Metaphysics series aims to provide a safe house for such thinking amidst the demoralizing caution and prudence of professional academic philosophy. We do not aim to bridge the analytic-continental divide, since we are equally impatient with nail-filing analytic critique and the continental reverence for dusty textual monuments. We favor instead the spirit of the intellectual gambler, and wish to discover and promote authors who meet this description. Like an emergent recording company, what we seek are traces of a new metaphysical 'sound' from any nation of the world. The editors are open to translations of neglected metaphysical classics, and will consider secondary works of especial force and daring. But our main interest is to stimulate the birth of disturbing masterpieces of twenty-first century philosophy.

Gabriel Yoran

The Interfact: On Structure and Compatibility in Object-Oriented Ontology

OPEN HUMANITIES PRESS

London, 2021

First edition published by Open Humanities Press 2021

Copyright © 2021 Gabriel Yoran

Freely available online at http://openhumanitiespress.org/books/titles/the-interfact

Design by Katherine Gillieson
Cover Illustration by Tammy Lu

The cover illustration is copyright Tammy Lu 2021, used under a
Creative Commons By Attribution license (CC-BY).

PRINT ISBN 978-1-78542-099-3
PDF ISBN 978-1-78542-098-6

OPEN HUMANITIES PRESS

Open Humanities Press is an international, scholar-led open access publishing collective whose mission is to make leading works of contemporary critical thought freely available worldwide. More at http://openhumanitiespress.org

Contents

Acknowledgments

Many people were involved in the creation of this book. I could not have done this without them. Foremost, I want to thank Florian Hadler for his early encouragement, and Nicole des Bouvrie, whose intellectual vigor is an inspiration. I owe great thanks to James Batcho, Jonathan Bennett Bonilla, Lukas F. Hartmann, Timothy Morton, Wolfgang Schirmacher, Ruben Schneider, and Siegfried Zielinski, all of whom have helped me in unique ways. I am grateful to Sigi Jöttkandt at Open Humanities Press for bringing this book to life and to the reviewers, whose thoughtful and thorough feedback has served this work well. Thanks go to my parents and Benjamin Gabriel for their emotional and intellectual support. And finally, I am especially grateful to the ever so patient and generous Graham Harman, whose ideas I had the privilege to build on (and wrangle with) throughout this book.

Introduction

Since object-oriented ontology (ooo) grants ontological priority to objects, it should have an easy time *referring* to objects. But this is not the case. What we mean when we talk about an object is surprisingly hard to say. What do we mean when we say *this object?* Simply by positing this question we find ourselves in the death strip between ontology and epistemology. For in an object-oriented ontology, is there even a legitimate *we*, a human, social subject? The problem of referring to objects, the problem of haecceity, is what concerns us in this work. In order to discuss this problem we will have to navigate the outer realms of object-oriented ontology.

"What can I know? What must I do? What may I hope for? What is man?"[1] The four Kantian questions, as universal as they seem, pivot around the I. All knowledge gained is knowledge only in the cognitive relation between acts of consciousness and an outside world, which is deemed more or less inaccessible. Every ethical demand is demanded of an I. Every hope experienced is experienced by an I. Kant holds that answering these three questions will inevitably lead to an answer of the fourth: what is man? And it is again an I who questions what it is. The Western world lives in the Kantian horizon. It pivots around the I.

Speculative realists set out to change that. While not representing a unified theory, this line of thought encompasses different non-anthropocentric positions striving to, in Ray Brassier's words, "re-interrogate or to open up a whole set of philosophical problems that were taken to have been definitively settled by Kant, certainly, at least, by those working within the continental tradition."[2] Since overcoming the human as the epistemic center of the cosmos necessarily leads to both a speculative stance and a more or less realist position, speculative realism is a feasible term. In accordance with the tradition in which Kant named metaphysics "a wholly isolated speculative cognition of reason,"[3] speculative realism merely makes the nature of its task obvious by naming it accordingly.

The variant of speculative realism which will be analyzed in more detail in this work is object-oriented philosophy (more often referred to as object-oriented ontology and thus abbreviated ooo), a theory of contemporary American philosopher Graham Harman, who also coined the term. Even though ooo is subsumed under the speculative realism movement, Harman claims to be "the only realist in speculative realism."[4]

Contrary to Heidegger's pejorative use of the term object, virtually all entities are objects in object-oriented ontology, including human subjects, Platonic ideas or even complex compound objects. A particularly systematic approach in this line of thought is Harman's "new fourfold," a model for the ways objects touch—or interact with—each other and also an analysis of traditional ontologies.[5] The new fourfold theory is not just about physical objects interacting with each other, which would be a mere physicalist exercise. It is about regarding nearly everything as objects and then discussing the relations between them, while elevating objects to a position where they are ontologically on the same level as the richest and deepest entities imaginable. Such objects lead an inaccessible life on the inside, and they do so independently of any consciousness witnessing this life. The quadruplicity refers to a complex set of relations that take place on the inside of every object and shape how the outside of an object appears to other objects. A particular problem this book touches on is how we can identify an object in the ooo sense as a specific object at all.

The speculative stance of object-oriented ontology poses a challenge to the anthropocentric epistemic tradition. We will analyze how ooo differs from other ontologies, which according to Harman either reduce the world to tiny material objects, to their outer relations or to a mere combination of those two. By starting to map the "basic landmarks and fault lines in the universe of objects," Harman launches an endeavor he calls ontography.[6] He suggests that "in several respects the model of ontography has begun to resemble that of particle physics,"[7] which could mislead readers into thinking of ooo as a naïve materialism or biologist reductionism, both of which are not the case. Also, ooo does not lead to a materialist determinism since its objects cannot be fully described (let alone replaced by their description) and their future cannot be completely forecast.

The quadruple object's concept of tensions crosses objects as they are being confronted by other objects (not just perceived by the human mind) and their reality with the shimmering relation between such objects and their qualities.[8] These tensions are already explored in contemporary art and our relations to it. Postmodern art theorists such as Umberto Eco hold that the relations works of art enter into are not pre-conceivable,[9] that works of art cannot be exhausted completely, thus holding back a surplus—a stance which applies to every real object in the quadruple object model. Works of art are generally accepted as being unified objects, but when related to the artist, other works of art, and of course to the spectator (reader, listener…) they tend to be granted a life of their own. We will make use of this position throughout this work in order to provide a more vivid understanding of object relations in general.

As with most philosophical terms, the term object is laden with different meanings, and quite a few enterprises have been undertaken to find alternative terminology that does not carry the burden of the object. As Ian Bogost notes, "an object implies a subject" as well as "materiality." So, in his "tiny ontology" he suggests the term "unit."[10] In this work however, we will stay with the term object, not least since it refers to ooo's surprising parallels with the concept of objects in a seemingly unrelated space: computer science.

ooo, even though this is most likely unintended, is a substance ontology developed under the impression of informatics. It "might be termed the first computational medium-based philosophy, even if it is not fully reflexive of its own historical context in its self-understanding of the computation milieu in which it resides."[11] It is "perhaps the first Internet or born-digital philosophy has certain overdetermined characteristics that reflect the medium within which [it has] emerged."[12] Such notions usually refer to the leading figures of speculative realism using blogs and social media to distribute their thoughts quickly and engage in lively discussions with the academic community online. ooo however has a deeper relation to the computational sphere: while Harman first publicly mentioned the term object-oriented philosophy in 1999,[13] object-oriented programming was already invented in the late 1960s—and the parallels between these two domains are noteworthy.

Working at the Norwegian Computing Center in Oslo, Ole-Johan Dahl und Kristen Nygaard in the 1960s conceived a new way of computer programming, in which what was separate before, namely data and functions, were molded into combined and somehow sealed logical units. Dahl and Nygaard named these units "objects" and the programming language they developed, Simula 67, is regarded the first to allow for software development following the paradigm of object-oriented programming (OOP).[14]

OOP has been in use for nearly five decades now, and while it is still a popular way of structuring software development projects large and small today, its critics have become more vocal. OOP's unnecessary complexity is just one of the issues computer language designers bring up: "The problem with object-oriented languages is they've got all this implicit environment that they carry around with them. You wanted a banana but what you got was a gorilla holding the banana and the entire jungle."[15] Regardless of OOP coming under fire lately, the striking parallels between the aesthetic and technological praxis of object-oriented programming on the one side and a new metaphysics on the other, promise a fruitful contribution to the ontographic project.

As a science investigating "the structure and properties (not specific content) of scientific information, as well as the regularities of scientific information activity, its theory, history, methodology and organization," informatics was defined in the 1960s.[16] Since then the task of informatics has been extended beyond the analysis of scientific information and deepened by performing this task using the means of computing. Thus, informatics today has become the science that investigates the structure and properties of information. The similarities between object-oriented programming and object-oriented ontology do not come as a surprise, given that informatics is traditionally occupied with metaphysics: both computer science and philosophy "do not address the materiality of things such as physics, they are not confined to the 'science of quantity'

(= mathematics)."[17] Since computer science strives to map reality onto computational structures, employing substance ontologies seems obvious. As computer science works on domain-specific models in order to find solutions to practical problems, employing models of the world, informatics is—like any proper science—applied metaphysics.

We will refer to concepts from informatics throughout this work, not just because of the namesake programming paradigm of object-oriented programming, but because two key figures, whose thinking will be used in this work to challenge ooo, employ notions of informatics or mathematics. While Quentin Meillassoux will only be covered briefly, Gilbert Simondon's work on individuation will be of more interest here. Simondon strove to unify technological and biological thinking in a common theory of information in order to explain individuation or the genesis of objects. His work is highly relevant for ooo as it extensively covers the question of objects as being or becoming (the latter being rejected by Harman as "gradualism"). According to contemporary scholar Miguel Penas López, Simondon held that "modern theory of information, as well as cybernetics, fails to grasp [the process of individuation] because they only take into account either its extreme terms (form-matter) or the message to be sent between them (signal), forgetting how these extremes can relate."[18] Simondon's demand on information theory was fulfilled in part with the advent of object-oriented programming (oop), which we will look into in chapter 2.

When one holds that the world is ultimately made of objects, those distinct and somehow independent entities, one question inevitably comes up: what do we mean when we say *this object*? The question of "thisness" or "haecceity" is the guiding question of this work. And again, the *we* is crucial.

Is it the epistemic or the ontological *we*? The epistemic *we* traditionally asks a question from a genuinely human perspective, be it social, historic or with some other relation to the human subject. It could be rephrased as: What do humans mean when they say *this*? Or more precisely: How do we as humans make sure we are actually referring to an object in ooo's sense? Where does an object begin and where does it end? Is this or that even an object at all? But trying to answer these questions alone misses the point, for different reasons in the two cases. In answering the epistemic question alone, we would betray the core principle of ooo, which aims to establish a speculative, non-anthropocentric stance. There are already many idealist or correlationist philosophies out there discussing how things relate to the human mind. Second, we will never know the answer to the questions of how many objects are out there, or where one object begins or ends—and this insecurity is a key part of ooo. Object-oriented philosopher Timothy Morton says he doesn't want to be the "object police": "ooo is about *how* things exist if they do. There might be just five things in the universe. Or five trillion. I have no idea."[19]

ooo is about *how* things exist, or to put it in ooo terms: it is about how objects *confront each other*. This is the ontological question: what happens when objects confront each other? Being true to ooo, our answer will necessarily span the realms of ontology and epistemology. Objects among each other, and without human epistemic activity of any kind, do not just *confront* each other, but they necessarily take part in each other's *epistemic* individuation. While ooo holds that objects are ontologically exhaustive without any context, their sensual parts are always a co-creation of at least two objects: in confronting each other, objects perform some kind epistemic process which eventually feeds back into the reality of the objects involved. The present work wants to establish this idea, deducing it from the principles of ooo, not from a correlationist stance.

We will start by giving quick introductions to both object-oriented ontology and the new fourfold object model introduced by Harman (chapter 1). This is followed by a necessarily short account of object-oriented programming (oop) including a discussion of the traits both concepts share (chapter 2). Using Gadamer, Putnam, and Kripke we apply oop's interface concept to the question of object identification (chapter 3), which will lead us to the problem of object genesis. How objects come into being relates to the question of how objects integrate into a larger fabric of objects, which will be discussed in chapter 4, where we will eventually use Simondon to start making some modest suggestions for how to extend Harman's fourfold model to better account for object genesis and integration.

In chapter 5 we will discuss two alternative realist philosophies, deviating from ooo in crucial points. While Penas López' attempt to infuse ooo with Simondonian process philosophy supports the interface concept we propose, Meillassoux's "mathematism" will be rejected using the lessons learned from the practice of digitization in chapter 5. Returning one last time to the question of object identification through integration into a larger fabric, we will touch on the problem of distortion in object-relations, which seems antithetical to ooo in its absoluteness. In his first book outlining "elements of an object-oriented philosophy," *Tool-Being*, Harman agrees with Heidegger and Whitehead "that an entity is determined by the systematic attachments into which it enters. In other words, there is no absolute line in the sand between monad and global machine. Every entity displays both aspects."[20] We want to take up this thought when proposing the "interfact," conceiving of objects as *supporting* each other. In true ooo spirit, we ask the reader to suspend their disbelief and speculatively regard epistemic processes as something objects perform when confronting each other, and as something that is real and thus yields a stable yet emergent reality. Eventually this work will present the notion that objects supporting each other is at the basis of what we call facts.

Chapter 1

Identifying Objects in OOO

Patrolling the Borders of Epistemic Capacity

Any metaphysics in the classic Aristotelian sense makes statements about things beyond the physically observable world. Since this was interpreted (for example by empiricism) as meaning that metaphysics makes unprovable statements, the metaphysical task was deemed senseless, a position that has dominated (continental) philosophy since Kant's time. The question of what is at the root of everything was regarded as unanswerable, since every statement one could make would just be perspectival. The fact that there cannot be an absolute statement from a human perspective led to a halt in metaphysics and to a flourishing of relativist postmodernism: Continental philosophy stopped doing metaphysics and instead focused on a multitude of stories.[21]

But what does "being at the root of everything that is" mean? Does it mean that there is one entity that generates everything else? This position puts God or the *apeiron*, an all-encompassing substance of the Pre-Socratics, at the ontological root of the world. In either case, it would mean that somehow everything is connected or everything is one thing, a position known as monism.

Object-oriented ontology holds that there is nothing like a root of everything, but that reality is made up of distinct entities or objects, which have a real core, independently of human perception (or any other kind). Strong idealist positions completely deny the existence of a thing in its own right. The term "idealism" encompasses very different positions, but what they all have in common is that what is, is reduced to a mere relation to human consciousness. Idealists hold that every proposition is always just a proposition by human consciousness, and is therefore always only relative. As Harman holds, Kant's "Copernican revolution" in the *Critique of Pure Reason* did not remove the I from the center of the cosmos. According to Harman's reading, Kant actually fixed the I in its center by introducing a seemingly inescapable epistemic relativism—the inaccessible thing-in-itself. This move, Harman holds, leads to the opposite of what the introduction of the Copernican planetary system did: the thing-in-itself exists only from a human perspective. "For the only function of things-in-themselves in Kant's philosophy is to haunt human knowledge as a sort of ghoulish residue. The major defect is that no discussion is possible about how things-in-themselves relate to each other."[22] So all knowledge gained becomes relative to the I. Objects would not have a life of their own.

Both Hegel and Heidegger, to name but a few, attack the subject of knowledge as in itself a fiction by holding that there is no "I know." However, they do not elevate non-conscious entities onto the same ontological level as human consciousness with the same rigor as object-oriented ontology does. The philosophical self-limitation of this kind of relativism stems from what is regarded a fundamental epistemological problem, which only brings forth what contemporary French philosopher Quentin Meillassoux calls "correlationist" philosophies.[23]

Under the term "correlationism" various schools of thought are subsumed: they differ in detail, but all take into account the alleged impossibility of speaking about things outside the mind, since by doing so these things are already inside the mind. Correlationist schools of thought differ in how they handle this correlate. But they do not question the necessity of thinking in a correlation of human and world (or language and world, for that matter). They hold it is the only acceptable way of thinking about the world—in correlation with the I. Therefore, correlationism encompasses all kinds of idealist (or anti-realist) thinking, from Kant's impossibility of capturing the thing-in-itself to constructivism. Accepting the fundamental human limits on making any true absolute statement, the only acceptable solution seems to be to withdraw oneself to the safe haven of relativist or perspectival positions, giving up on the project of metaphysics altogether.

Contemporary analytic philosophers like McGinn or Brüntrup hold that the specifics of the human epistemic apparatus, consisting of only two ways of cognition (mental introspection of the stream of consciousness and external observation), don't allow us to seek a "metaphysical unity" that would reside beyond human epistemic capacity, thus rendering any ontographic enterprise nonsensical.[24] This stance assumes that metaphysics as a task would only be successful if a kind of unity—a philosophical world formula of sorts—were the goal, and implicitly rules out the possibility of not finding a unity because there might be none. Brüntrup holds that a contemporary anti-realist position still needs to limit knowledge and truth to a mere "perspective." However, he adds the codicil "on a human scale," hinting at the possibility of something along the lines of a God-like scale, leaving a door open at the borders of human epistemic capacity.[25]

This border seems to be in need of constant patrolling. Meillassoux brings up the example of the contemporary scientist, who would add the codicil "for humans—or even: for the human scientist"[26] to any kind of statement, and would therefore reduce any knowledge we gain to a mere perspectival stance, making the modern scientist an idealist. So even scientists, with all their "objective" measurements and peer-reviewed experiments, seemingly cannot escape what Meillassoux calls the correlationist circle.[27]

Though one might still be able to speak about these ominous things outside the mind (whether they exist or not), the correlationist circle demands that one will always have to consider all such statements as relative to oneself. One cannot make statements that do not automatically have oneself in some way as a part of them. "Everything is relative," the common sense of modernity: Leibniz demonstrating the relativity of space, Einstein showing the relativity of time, Freud describing the relativity of the conscious mind, which secretly depends on the unconscious. There is seemingly no escaping the correlation. It even invades language: the position that every knowledge is always mediated through language, also known as the linguistic turn, holds that language marks an epistemic barrier. As

Wittgenstein famously put it: "The limits of my language mean the limits of my world."[28]

If one accepts the correlationist circle, one must also accept that one cannot gain access to any absolute knowledge. For the correlationist it is unnecessary to share Slavoj Žižek's extreme position of there not being a world at all outside the mind, since "the correlationist need not be committed to the thesis that there is no being apart from thought. Indeed, most correlationists are committed to the thesis that there is something other than thought… The correlationist merely argues that we have no access to these beings that are apart from thought and can therefore only speak of being as it is for-us."[29]

Contemporary German philosopher Markus Gabriel also holds that "there is no world," not from a radical idealist perspective, but from a realistic one: Gabriel holds that everything else exists, just not "the world."[30] According to Gabriel we cannot talk about the world, since if this were possible, the world would need to be a part of the world, located for example in our mind. But the world is not part of the world. For Gabriel, what is meant when talking about the world is just one "field of sense" ("Gegenstandsbereich"), and in the case of the "world" (or "universe") it is specifically the physical field of sense.[31] The world for Gabriel is the field of sense of all fields of sense. He thus basically criticizes the linguistic fallacy of calling the totality of everything that exists the "world," and assuming thereby that there is only this one universe of discourse. Gabriel does not hold that there is no world, but that there are multiple worlds of discourse, some discrete, some overlapping. These universes of discourse bear some resemblance to objects in object-oriented ontology. ooo does not hold that there are no perspectives, nor does it postulate absolute human access to the totality of what is. Rather, it extends this impossibility of total access to anything or anyone.

ooo does not put one entity at the root of everything, nor does it make everything one. Instead of a root, ooo postulates what Levi Bryant calls the "democracy of objects."[32] Instead of the world pivoting around the I, in object-oriented ontology objects pivot around other objects, a human consciousness being only one of these objects. These objects interact, they "confront" or "touch," and they can do so with or without humans (or anyone or anything else) perceiving this interaction. Object-oriented ontology is realist, but not in a naïve scientistic way. But how can one make truthful propositions about something we cannot observe? How can we leave the safe haven of correlationism? How can we justify talking about objects without correlating? How can we justify talking about absolutes?

In an attempt to show the problem of breaking out of the correlationist circle, Meillassoux calls upon specific physical artifacts. In *After Finitude*, he notes that "empirical science is today capable of producing statements about events anterior to the advent of life as well as consciousness."[33] By using the technology of carbon dating, it is possible to date with great precision when a certain thing, for example the bone of a dinosaur, came into being. Meillassoux calls these objects stemming from a time before human consciousness (or even life at all), "archefossils." He calls statements referring to this time "ancestral" statements.

What is the problem posed by the archefossil's existence? One might argue that an idealist could not accept the existence of such a fossil, since they only accept an outside world in correlation with the mind. If there were no human minds around during the era of the dinosaurs, how could this fossil come into existence? A strategy for keeping idealism intact is to argue that the archefossil is something that appears to us today as something being in existence since before the advent of humankind (or life). This stance might sound promising for creationists who would hold that God made us falsely believe that the archefossil is seemingly older than earth (which according to their worldview is only 6,000 years of age) to challenge our faith. The idea that such an illusion would be in the world just to fool humankind represents the very anthropocentric view that speculative realism wants to overcome.

Another strategy for coping with the archefossil would be to establish another entity as the witness of ancestral events (most likely God). But if we did this, Meillassoux holds, we would not be able to speak of correlationism anymore.[34] The correlate is always a relation between a human subject and the world. If some other entity is needed to "witness" an ancestral event, we are not talking about correlationism, but some kind of metaphysics, for example religion. Every philosophy that needs something or someone, a God or a conscience, to witness events in order for them actually to take place, poses a centrist view that does not account for independently existing and interacting objects.

Arguments for a Modern Realism

Covering the realist criticism of a complex and historically changing philosophy such as idealism is beyond the scope of this work (as is the discussion of whether the dichotomy between realism and idealism is actually meaningful). We want to focus instead on the arguments ooo brings forth in order to justify revisiting the seemingly outdated philosophy of realism—and how the "strange realism" it proposes differs from its traditional scientist or naïve variants.

The first strategy ooo employs is criticizing its reductionist alternatives: Harman rereads the history of Western philosophy by analyzing how objects are treated. He identifies three basic strategies of dismissing objects as the basic ontological building blocks of philosophy: reducing them to their (smaller) parts, which he calls "undermining," reducing them to their (larger) relations, named "overmining," or a combination of both ("duomining").[35]

Undermining

Undermining is a strategy of looking for the smaller parts that make up the objects as they appear to us: a table therefore would only be its molecules, which would "actually" comprise only atoms, quarks, strings, or whatever the smallest entity currently being known in physics is. Undermining is a strategy of breaking things apart to find their truth—and thereby denying any truth to the table as a table. It is obvious that this method would need to be applied over and over indefinitely, and still truth would not be found. Many processes in the world take place on higher levels like the sociological, psychological, even biological, and it is not the tiniest parts that contain the truth about an object's reality. Undermining means stating that objects are "a mere surface effect of some deeper force."[36] According to Harman, this materialist position of accepting only the existence of smallest parts, and claiming that they exhaust an object in its totality, leads to a world of stasis. For since all objects are already fully expressed (or exhausted) any possibility of change would be ruled out. Undermining does not account for emergence (and therefore might also lead to determinism).

Overmining

Overmining philosophies however hold that objects are only manifestations in the mind,[37] which makes all of them correlationists. Overmining can be found in lines of thought as different as empiricism and constructivism and can be broken down into three kinds:

1. Empiricism is a classical overmining philosophy holding that objects are constructed in the mind: according to the overmining strategy of empiricism, objects are only constituted by human habit—and human habit is what binds separate features like redness, sweetness, coldness etc. together to what is then "overminingly" called an apple. Harman calls the idea of experiencing the world as "isolated points of quality" (or "pixels") a "pure fiction" since "what we encounter in experience are unified objects."[38] This is because the allegedly separate qualities are already informed or affected by the object as a whole. One cannot experience "glossiness" or "mirroring" as such, but only glossiness of a surface or the reflection in another object like a mirror.

2. Strong anti-realism is overmining as well since it holds that there are no objects outside the mind. As Berkeley famously put it: "*esse is percipii*"[39] (to be is to be perceived).

3. Correlationist anti-realism overmines as well, since it holds that we can only think in terms of a correlation between consciousness the and world.

Duomining

Today undermining and overmining often appear in the same line of thought: this strategy, named "duomining," reduces objects to their parts while holding that even this knowledge of the tiniest parts is just a construction of reality. What we experience as objects would therefore not be real, since reality is only to be found in tiny parts, which again are just an illusion. This is scientific materialism par excellence: a paradox and a highly unsatisfactory strategy. Nevertheless, it is probably one of the most popular lines of thought today.

When Harman refers to objects as "what we encounter in experience" or as "the simple fact that something is or seems to be one thing," the realist speaks.[40] But how can we use our own experience as a valid starting point for developing a metaphysics? What are the strategies that justify making absolute statements? Let us look at the strategies that justify realist positions.

Reversing the Correlation

ooo strives to reverse the correlation. Harman was among the first to read French sociologist Bruno Latour as a philosopher.[41] Latour's actor-network theory inspired object-oriented ontology by granting mundane things a dramatically more important role (especially in philosophy, which is usually more occupied with the human being, the mind, the cosmos, or God). Latour protests the ontological separation of human beings and everything else by positing that in praxis humans and things (or mind and world) have been mixed up all the time, their interaction being crucial for the development of humankind. Latour holds that it is specific to modernity to compulsively separate areas of discourse, even though they overlap in reality. He gives the example of French biologist Louis Pasteur, whose discovery (and naming) of microbes changed the scientific worldview and influenced the lives of people around the world by establishing the politics of hygiene. In Pasteur: guerre et paix des microbes, Latour describes the *Pasteurization of France* (this also being the book's English title), namely the overlapping areas of discourse as different as biology, politics, medicine, city planning, and others.[42] The discovery of microbes illustrates a serious flaw in correlationist thinking, namely its implicit unidirectionalism: while from a correlationist point of view it seems clear that microbes only exist in a correlation with the human thinking of them, and thus only came into existence the moment they were "discovered," correlationism is a two-way road travelled in only one direction. In a provocative thought experiment, Harman imagines Latour's "evil twin" holding as follows:

Microbes have always existed, or at least have existed since
their emergence on our hot planet billions of years ago. By
contrast, humans are fragile, ephemeral, and not of especial
importance. Microbes have existed all along—but only when
Pasteur discovered them did he begin to exist. Only after
1864 did Pasteur exist all along! But not the microbes, whose
existence all along is beyond all dispute.[43]

The tremendous success of Western idealism has led us to think
correlations in only one direction: pointing from the human conscious to
the non-human outside world. Reversing this direction to point from the
microbe to Pasteur shows the arbitrariness of this line of thought.

Thinking the Unthought

Another strategy Harman employs to justify a renaissance of realism is
exposing the linguistic fallacy in terms of the impossibility of thinking
what is outside the mind: Harman refers to Plato's dialogue *Meno* to prove
that the correlationist circle's seeming inescapability is actually a linguistic
fallacy. Socrates sums up the (alleged) paradox that comes up in his
dialogue with Meno: "A man cannot search either for what he knows or for
what he does not know[.] He cannot search for what he knows—since he
knows it, there is no need to search—nor for what he does not know, for he
does not know what to look for."[44] Socrates himself explained that though
"we have some grasp of the subject," we never have an "exhaustive" one.[45]
As Harman puts it: "(a) You cannot think the unthought while thinking it
(because then it would be a thought), and (b) you also cannot think of the
unthought while not thinking of it (for obvious reasons). Therefore, (c) there
can be no thinking of the unthought."[46] Harman holds that "thought" here
has two very different meanings, mixed up in the derivation: thinking as
making something "present to the mind" does not equal thinking as pointing
"at its reality insofar as it lies beyond its presence to the mind."[47]

In a way, the difference of reality and its presence to the mind can
also be found in the concept of pointers in computer programming: the
structure of modern programming languages distinguishes between actual
data stored in the computer's memory (which would correspond to a reality

beyond its presence to the mind) and a "pointer" which consists only of the address of (or reference to) the above-mentioned data, therefore "pointing" at a place somewhere else. The pointer illustrates thinking as pointing to (or referencing) an outside reality instead of being identical to it or even replacing it in a way that makes outside reality a mere fiction (as strong correlationists hold). The pointer in computer science corresponds to Kripke's concept of names as "rigid designators"—designators completely independent from the content to which they refer.[48]

Always a Distance

The strategy most consequential in terms of its influence on ooo is in pointing out the arbitrariness of the human/world rift. As realists, both Harman and Gabriel hold that the seemingly unsurpassable rift between human consciousness and the outside world is completely random. More specifically the Cartesian dualism, posing that there are only two substances, the thinking substance and the material substance, is what is regarded as random. Why are there only two substances, not three, ten or ten thousand? Harman holds that "it hardly matters whether the gap is preserved (Kant) or purportedly overcome (phenomenology). The point is that no other rifts are taken into account."[49] And since ooo rejects the monist idea of everything being one or made up of one substance only, Harman suggests that there is a multitude of substances. The price to pay for an endless amount of substances however is that this opens up not just one rift, but an endless number of rifts: since every object is its own substance, ooo tears open rifts between all objects.

A central element of object-oriented ontology is describing if, how, and to what extent at all these rifts are surpassed: as concerns the epistemic capacity not just of human consciousness, but also those of other entities (as esoteric as this might sound at first); Harman rejects the "post-Kantian obsession with a relational gap between people and objects"[50] not by removing this gap, but by introducing gaps between all objects. As Ian Bogost put it, in object-oriented ontology "there is always a distance."[51]

Kant held that "if one removes the special condition of our sensibility from it, then the concept of time also disappears, and it does not adhere to the objects themselves, rather merely to the subject that intuits them."[52]

Time as something put into phenomena by human experience (like colors) is not rejected by ooo, but rather is extended to all confrontations between objects: all such confrontations produce sensual objects, which are under the influence of the real objects participating in them. This is one of the reasons why ooo is regarded a "strange"[53] realism.[54]

A First Look at Object-Poles and Tensions

The definition of an object in ooo is complex: every material, immaterial or fictitious entity is an object. Objects can be, but do not have to be, real in a physical sense. Not all objects are "equally real," even though they are all equally objects.[55] The term "real object" must not be confused with the reality of a material object.

So, objects are not limited to durable physical units, but rather include compound objects like hammers, and more complex compounds such as the European Union. Events are objects, as are unicorns and even square circles. (Time and space are special cases. We will look into these phenomena in detail later.) Human consciousness is an object among objects. It is ontologically not superior to any other object, and therefore relations between non-human objects are not treated differently "from human perception of them."[56] Even though the interactions that human consciousness is capable of are very different from those of rivers and stones, they are not granted a higher ontological position—ooo's ontology is flat. This leads to objects interacting with each other without the need of human consciousness witnessing such interactions. These interactions are indirect ("vicarious causation") and vary wildly.[57]

When treating all these very different entities mentioned as objects, the question arises: what is it that makes an object an object in the first place? While Heidegger differentiated between the mundane object and the more sublime "thing," and the Leibnizian theory of monads rather randomly declared some things objects but others not, ooo treats all these entities the same.[58] Objects can be mundane or sublime, they are still objects. The quadruple object model does not aim for a synthesis of existing theories of substance. It is a realist approach, which might nevertheless appear idealist to the reader. The reason for this is the definition of objects as "anything having a unified reality that is autonomous from its wider context and its own pieces."[59] The object "the river Rhine," for example, is autonomous from its own pieces, because even though its precise physical configuration changes permanently, the water molecules are in constant flux, and the location of the riverbed doesn't stay in the same place if observed for decades and centuries. Nevertheless, it is still the river Rhine.[60] But what is this "it"—and for whom?

One might think that the primary identifier of the object named "Rhine" is its name. From a semiotic point of view, the name of any object is just arbitrary and conventional. Instead of the Rhine, which kept its name for centuries, let us look at less durable identifiers, such as Berlin street names. The street known as Danziger Straße in the Prenzlauer Berg area was named Dimitroffstraße (after a Bulgarian communist leader) from 1950 through 1995. When the street was named back to Danziger Straße, what happened to the object formerly known as Dimitroffstraße? The name was changed and the object that is somehow related to the topographic structure is now known under a different name. The name is merely part of the street's wider context; it is a unique identifier on a Berlin map, necessary to differentiate this street from any other.

So, the name is not the primary identifier of an object. That's because there is no such thing as a primary identifier of an object: the object itself is its own primary, unique and sole identifier in the cosmos. Being an object "does not mean to possess X number of qualities, since these qualities serve at best as instruction for how to identify it from the outside."[61] So the object, which is now named Danziger Straße, is exactly what it needs to "enact the reality in the cosmos"[62] of which Danziger Straße alone is capable. This explains why an object cannot be duplicated, because any copy would enact a different reality than its original—thus, no two objects can be alike.[63]

The impossibility of having multiple identical objects is confirmed by the fact that every relation forms a new object. This trait is crucial to understanding object-oriented ontology. Even if the same physical tree appeared before two different minds, these relations would mean two different objects. This is where the fourfold structure of the quadruple object comes into play. In every object, there are four "poles."

The Sensual Object

The sensual object, which is basically a more accessible term for the traditional, but misleading term of the "intentional" object, describes an object as it appears to another object. In the case of one of the two objects being a human mind, for example, it describes an object as it appears in the human being's mind. But since these appearances change all the time without the object changing beyond the possibility of identifying it as the same object, there is a tension between the object and its own sensual qualities.

Sensual Qualities

Sensual qualities are the constantly shifting aspects of the sensual object. But the totality of these qualities does not constitute an object, not even a sensual one. The tension between the sensual object as the unified entity that appears before another object (e.g. the mind) and its ever-changing qualities is a constitutive part of the quadruple object: this tension represents the fact that something can change qualitatively without becoming "something else." While the object as a whole is a digital concept, binary, and discretely differentiated from other objects, with no allowance for grey values, the tensions between object-poles are an analog concept: this is where we find space for subtle and virtually unlimited variations.

One might think of an analog auditory experience such as listening to a piano recital at a concert hall. The amount of (musical) data with which the ear is being confronted virtually unlimited in terms of acoustic resolution and musical complexity. And even though one might experience the concert differently depending on one's unlimited variability of moods, the concerto one experiences is exactly one object, which cannot be reconstructed from the sum of its parts. Even if the totality of data needed to reconstruct the recital was available and recordable (which is not the case), its reconstruction would be just that: a reconstruction, in another space-time and in another context, one's mood will probably be different—and we can say with certainty that this duplicate is definitely not the same object as the original concert. But a certain caveat has to be stressed as concerns the digital/analog metaphor. While a digital copy of a digital object produces a perfectly identical twin, the copies' representation as a quadruple object is not the same object as the original at all. As the recorded and reproduced piano concerto example showed, the quadruple object theory holds that everything is original all the time—and a reproduction never exhausts its original.

The tension between a sensual object and its sensual qualities stems from Husserl's phenomenological observations. An object does stay the same in a way, but it also changes; a house which is looked at in a mood of joy in the bright sunlight appears the same, but also different when seen at night in a gloomy mood. This is why the tension between sensual objects and their sensual qualities in a quadruple object is called "time." "When we speak of time in the everyday sense, what we are referring to is a remarkable interplay of stability and change. In time, the objects of sense do not seem motionless and fixed but are displayed as encrusted with shifting features."[64]

Initially taking cues from Husserl's phenomenology seems counterproductive when idealism is to be overcome. But Harman holds that phenomenology is not just another form of idealism, but introduces a tension that can be used as a cornerstone for the quadruple object model.[65] Husserl, as a philosopher of intentional objects, holds that we experience qualities "as if they emanated from an underlying object."[66] With Harman stressing Husserl's discovery of a tension "between intentional objects and the qualities that emanate from them" and that "no such tension can be found in previous idealisms,"[67] phenomenology sounds well-nigh realist.

After having given a first description of sensual object and sensual qualities, we have a rough idea of two of the four object-poles. Since both sensual object and qualities are just representing the surface, the interface, there must be more to constitute a "real" object. We might use a parallel from computer languages to introduce the "real" object and its qualities, which will constitute the other half of the quadruple object.

The Real Object

The real object represents the inner workings of the object, the totality of the object's enactability of its reality in the cosmos. The real object is inexhaustible in any sensual relation (by what was described as the interface in the computational object), since it is an unlimited repository for everything that could be realized through the object (the "surplus"). The tension resulting from the real object and its sensual qualities stem from how sensual qualities change, "the radiation of ever new profiles from [the object's] surface," while the real object stays the same. Harman's reading of Heidegger's tool-analysis informs this duality: "The withdrawn or subterranean hammer is a concealed unit, but one that emits sensual qualities into the phenomenal sphere."[68]

The tension between the real object and its sensual qualities represent an "interplay of relation and non-relation," named "space."[69] Harman holds that space, in the general meaning of the term, is neither just the site of relation nor non-relation, but both: space is what separates and what unites. There is no distance beyond which one could speak of separation; there is always a potential for closeness, but even the closest relation in space will not exhaust an object in its totality. And sometimes one can even get a better perception of an object from a distance. This is why Heidegger's tool-analysis[70] convinced Harman that "the correlationist standpoint is wrong. … The fact that we can allude to concealed hammers by way of language or thought does not entail that the hammers are exhausted by such allusion."[71]

Real Qualities

Real qualities are probably the most problematic object-pole. While it is easy to understand that beneath mere surface effects a "real" object resides, which cannot be exhausted completely, and while it is a generally acceptable idea that there are tensions between a sensual object and its ever-changing qualities, it is far harder to accept why an entity that withdraws from any access has to be viewed as separate from its qualities, which should be just as inaccessible as the object itself.

In order to make this idea more palpable, we return to Danziger Straße. If there is no primary identifier for an object except for the object itself and the relations of object poles are in constant flux, we cannot identify objects at all, since everything sinks into an unidentifiable indeterminate lump (perhaps an all-encompassing entity like the *apeiron*). But this is not the case. If objects exist and can be identified, and the reality they enact is their identifier, then something about an object must be stable—and this is where the tension between the real object and its real qualities come into play. Harman calls for the symmetry needed in the model (having two sensual poles seemingly asks for two real poles). He also questions threefold structures as providing too easy of a way out (thesis, antithesis, synthesis might come to mind). The quadruple object however offers no relief—all the poles in an object are defined by the ongoing tensions with every other pole. The more convincing argument appears to be that the essence of an object is allowed some flexibility without losing its identity: it follows logically that the identity of an object is not a rigid concept, but—again—a tension. The real object allows for ever changing real qualities. This is why the tension between a real object and real quality in object-oriented ontology is called "essence." Real qualities in the quadruple object are not mobile universals, but qualities formed by the object to which they belong.[72]

But the quadruple object conception, as rigid it may seem at first glance, leaves space for the open, the unknown, or—as Harman puts it—the "surplus." Objects at their core are unknowable, they cannot be exhausted from the outside. In a Heideggerian move, Harman declares that they are "units that both display and conceal a multitude of traits."[73] They enter into relations to their own qualities. They enter into relations with other objects, exposing some of their qualities to other objects, like the human mind. But they all conceal some of their qualities, which makes then inexhaustible.

Giving an example from early Islamic theology, Harman describes fire and cotton as two objects making indirect contact by the hand of God.[74] In this case of "occasionalism" (as in actions being solely the occasion for God to enable them), fire can only burn cotton because it is God who makes the connection between the two objects. But even though God connects these two objects, the two objects do not exhaust each other. Fire can destroy cotton, but it doesn't need to interact with every aspect of the cotton to do so. Fire doesn't "require" the cotton's color, its material qualities for the production of apparel, or its softness. The interaction is not complete, but object-oriented ontology holds that that no interaction ever is. Even though objects interact with other objects all the time, including the human mind interacting with the objects outside the human mind, there is no chance of exhausting such an interaction (or relation). There is always something left unrealized. Otherwise, if all kinds of relations were always already realized, we would live in a world of stasis. ooo holds that without the surplus of the real, nothing new could come into it the world, and change would be impossible. Hence, the surplus serves as an inexhaustible repository of the future.

Chapter 2

Objects in Code

Parallels

"Computational metaphors share a lot of similarity in object-oriented software to the principles expressed by [ooo's] speculations about objects as objects,"[75] David M. Berry holds. There are astonishing parallels between object-oriented ontology and object-oriented programming, even though the former only borrowed the name from the latter.[76] These similarities will be explored in this chapter.

When object-oriented programming was invented, the dominant approach to computer programming was imperative or procedural. Imperative programming means conveying computational statements that directly alter the state of the program. A program designed in this way works, roughly, by linearly processing a list of functions step by step. When these statements are grouped into semantic units, or "procedures," one can speak of procedural programming. Procedures are used to group commands in a computer program in order to make large programs more easily maintainable. Groups of statements also make code reusable, since the same set of statements can be invoked again and again. It also makes code more flexible, since parameters can be handed to a procedure for it to process. Parameters can be thought of as values handed to functions (the x in f(x)). While the function follows the same logics, the operation's result depends on the parameters passed.

These improvements however were not sufficient to handle complex computational tasks such as weather forecasts. Tasks like this require simulations. And even though Alan Shapiro mockingly notes in a Baudrillardian comment that "the commercialized culture of the USA is substantially not a real world anymore: it is already a simulation. Object-oriented programming is a simulation of the simulation,"[77] the necessity of simulating weather systems or financial markets called for more sophisticated strategies to structure computer programs. Instead of grouping lists of statements into procedures and have these statements directly manipulate a program's state, object-oriented programming offers a vicarious approach. Computational statements and data are being bundled together in objects. These objects are being closed off to the rest of the program, and can only be accessed indirectly by means of defined interfaces. Under this new programming paradigm, computer programmers became object designers, forced to come up with an object-oriented ontology for the world they wanted to map into the computer's memory.

The invention of object-orientation made object-oriented computer languages a necessity. The available computer languages did not possess the grammar necessary to describe objects and their relations. It becomes clear that "computer language" or "programming language" are misleading terms. These languages are products of human invention. They are human-designed, human-understandable languages, which computers can process in order to fulfill certain tasks. Designing a programming language is an attempt at producing the toolset for future developers to solve as yet unanticipated problems, sometimes in ways that were previously inconceivable. Object-oriented ontologies in informatics are pragmatic and open. They are realist in the sense of being a useful system of denotators of things outside the computer (or the programming language). They aim at reusable program code, which only needs to be written once, so that problems do not need to be solved twice and errors do not have to be fixed in multiple places. Thus, the programming language designer's task is meta-pragmatic: designing a language as a tool for others to build tools to eventually fulfill certain tasks. Object-orientation discards lists of statements in favor of objects as the locus of "problem solving," to use a Simondonian term. Simondon's notion of the individual describes objects as "agents of compatibilization," solving problems between different "orders of magnitude."[78] With this notion Simondon anticipated the object in object-oriented programming; or at the very least, the actual implementation of objects in OOP proves to be aligned with the traits of the individual Simondon described.

Object-oriented programming became so widely adopted partly because it is close to the everyday experience of objects. It also makes strong use of hierarchies, another everyday concept. Objects may remain identifiable and stable from the outside, even when their interior changes dramatically. The "open/closed principle" is evidence of this: a component, not necessarily an object, needs to be open for future enhancement, but closed with regard to its already exposed interfaces. This closure ensures that other components that depend on the component can rely on the component's functionality displayed earlier; unexpected changes in behavior need to be prevented.[79] Being closed can be read as unity, as a certain stability of an object that makes it identifiable. Object-oriented programming, however, attains some of this stability by interweaving objects into a hierarchy, an idea that object-oriented ontology rejects.[80]

In both object-oriented programming and object-oriented ontology, objects are the dominant structural elements. In object-oriented programming, objects are supposed to be modeled after real-life objects, since the aim is to provide a sufficiently precise representation of the reality to be simulated. In practice, however, this undertaking often fails. Objects are being created in code for things that do not exist outside the program. Functionality is forced into object form even when the result is awkward and unsatisfying. A common problem that many software engineers who use object-oriented programming face is also found at the root of object-oriented ontology: we just do not know enough about objects in order to model worlds based on them. While OOO embraces this uncertainty, OOP naïvely denies it. Software engineers forced to use OOP must come up with a model of the world that will most likely be wrong, insufficient or counterproductive, while software developers employing the functional programming paradigm can focus on what needs to *happen*, not on how things *are*. As a result, alternative programming paradigms are gaining more interest lately, and new programming languages like Apple's Swift are designed that undogmatically mix different paradigms with the goal of always delivering the solution that's least error-prone for the use-case. But this should not be of any concern, since we are focusing on the multitude of traits that OOP and OOO share:

1. Objects are both systems' basic building blocks.

2. Objects can be anything from very simple to extremely complex.

3. Objects have an inner life that is not fully exposed to the outside.

4. Objects interact with other objects indirectly, and do not exhaust other objects completely.

5. Objects can destroy other objects.

6. Results of interactions between objects may or may not be predictable from outside an object.

7. Objects can contain objects.

8. Objects can change over time, but at the same time stay the same object in the sense of an identifiable entity.

9. No two objects are the same.

In this chapter, we will look into some of the more interesting parallels.

Objects as Unpredictable Bundles

The first programming language regarded as object-oriented was Simula 67, invented in the 1960s by Ole-Johan Dahl und Kristen Nygaard at the Norwegian Computing Center in Oslo. Simula 67 was designed as a formal language to describe systems with the goal of simulation (thus the name Simula, a composite of simulation and language). Simula already incorporated most major concepts of object-orientation. Most importantly, Dahl's and Nygaard's object definition still holds today: objects in object-oriented programming are bundles of properties (data) and code (behavior, logics, functions, methods). These objects expose a defined set of interfaces, which does not reveal the totality of the object's capabilities and controls the flow of information in and out of the object. These two specifics are subsumed under the "encapsulation" moniker.[81]

Objects in programming are another variant of "the ancient problem of the one and the many":[82] they exist as abstract definitions called "classes" or "object types," and as actual entities called "objects" or "instances." So, while a class is the Platonic description of an abstract object's properties and behavior, instances are the actual realization of such classes in a computer's memory.[83] There can be more than one instance of any class, and it is possible and even common for multiple instances of the same class to communicate with each other.

Let us look at a concrete example of the difference between procedural and object-oriented programming. In procedural programming, a typical function would be y=f(x), where f is the function performed on x and the function's result would be stored (returned) in the variable y. In object-orientation however, an object x would be introduced that would contain a method f. An interface would be defined that would allow for other objects to call f, using a specified pattern. And so, by invoking f, the member function being part of object x—or x.f() for short—the object, containing both data and functionality, stays within itself. In our case there is no return value, so no y to save the results of function f to. This is not necessary, as the object itself holds all the data it operates on.

Object-oriented programming has been criticized for the fact that the behavior of object methods (functions inside objects) is unpredictable when viewed from a strictly mathematical perspective. A mathematical function y=f(x) is supposed only to work on x and return the result in y. An object method however can also modify other variables inside its object and thus lead to unpredictable results. A function is supposed to return its result; an object method, however, modifies its object but does not necessarily return a copy of (or a pointer to) the whole modified object. When manipulating an object through one of its member functions, it is not known from the outside which effects this manipulation will have on the object internally. This means that the object's behavior following such a method call is not predictable from outside the object. While software developers generally try to prevent unpredictability, the object-oriented philosopher will hardly be surprised. It is a key characteristic of ooo that objects can behave in unpredictable ways, and that their interiority is sealed off from any direct access:

I think the biggest problem typically with object-oriented programming is that people do their object-oriented programming in a very imperative manner where objects encapsulate mutable state and you call methods or send messages to objects that cause them to modify themselves unbeknownst to other people that are referencing these objects. Now you end up with side effects that surprise you that you can't analyze.[84]

While in object-orientation data and operations performed on it need to be bundled into one object, the competing paradigm of functional programming means that operations and data are separated. In the functional programming language Haskell, for example, functions can only return values but cannot change the state of a program (as is the case in object-orientation).

The Platonic Class

While objects may have complex inner workings (code as well as data), they usually do not share all this information with other objects. An object exposes certain well-defined interfaces through which communication is possible. In line with object-orientation's original application, we want to discuss the key concepts of OOP using a simulation program. We will imagine a program simulating gravitational effects in our solar system. Such a program, if designed in an object-oriented way, would most definitely contain an object type—or Platonic "class"—representing a planet. Such a class would contain variables to describe a planet's physical and chemical properties like its diameter, atmosphere, age, current average temperature, its position in relation to the solar system's sun, etc. It would also contain methods used to manipulate class data. A method to change the average temperature (to account for the case of a slowly dying sun for example) would need to be implemented as well. In a solar system simulation, there would be multiple instances—objects—of the planet class; in the case of our solar system one would create objects for Earth, Jupiter, Saturn, etc.

The simulation would manipulate any planet's data by calling the object's respective method: for example, the one to change the planet's average temperature on the surface. The actual variable holding the average temperature itself would not be exposed to the object's outside. In this way, any interaction with the object must be mediated through the interface methods provided by the object. All interactions with an object become structured by this intermediate layer and can be checked for faulty inputs. Instead of directly changing the temperature on a planet to a value below absolute zero (which would be possible if direct access was given), the intermediate data setting method provides its own logic, and hence its own limitations, to prevent such a "misuse" of the object.

But all planets are different, and to take this into consideration in our simulation, we would need to set any instance's properties (data) accordingly. To do so, classes provide special "constructor" methods, which bring an instance of a class into existence. Constructors take parameters needed to initially construct an object and then create an instance accordingly. (To destroy objects, so-called "destructors" can be used as well.)

As mentioned, object-oriented programming differentiates between classes (object types) and objects.[85] What makes this parallel interesting is that it is an interplay between a fixed structure and free-floating accidents that constitutes an object. This interplay is what ooo deems an object's essence. So as not to stretch the analogies between ooo and oop too far, we should note that this interplay takes place on the inside of an object in ooo, while in oop it crosses borders between objects. But similar to the situation in ooo, objects can come into existence without actively enacting any reality. However, the object structure in oop (which we would call the counterpart to ooo's real-object-pole) defines what an object can do. This is to be understood as a potential and not as an exhaustive description of the object's capabilities. In oop, the instance of an object (what we have come to see as its real-qualities-pole) cannot be reduced to the object itself (the real-object-pole)—an object is therefore always more than its rigid structure. If the object has any interface with the outside, which is the case with most objects in oop, there is still no way to know the results of all possible interactions with the object.

Hierarchy and Inheritance

Let us assume that all the planets in our solar system simulation have been sufficiently defined. We would still need an object representing the sun. The sun is not a planet but a star, yet there are properties and probably methods that both share: something that all celestial bodies incorporate. Since its first incarnation in Simula 67, using the object-oriented programming paradigm is synonymous with organizing objects hierarchically in tree-like structures. Every object has at least one parent object (a superclass) and can have child objects (subclasses). An object then inherits all properties and methods of its superclass (or, in some cases, superclasses) and hands them and its own properties and methods down to its subclasses, which can then add additional properties and methods. So, both classes representing planets and suns should be derived from a superclass representing any celestial body. This celestial body class would then handle properties and methods shared by all its subclasses. Only methods and data necessary for more specific celestial bodies such as planets or stars would be defined in their respective subclasses. In OOP, a principle of reversed subsidiarity is at work: anything that can be handled at the highest, most abstract level is being handled there; only more specific tasks are being handled further down the object hierarchy.

OOP's terminology, which speaks of "parent classes," "child classes," and "inheritance," shows the hierarchical tradition in which OOP is rooted. Any object in the hierarchy "inherits" all traits from its parent object. Such a hierarchy has at its root an abstract object (CObject in Microsoft's MFC model), which only consists of abstract methods that make no statement about the specifics of this object at all. Such an object is rarely used directly by software developers, but only through one of its more concrete subclasses. But not all objects are part of such a hierarchy, like for example the CTime object in the MFC model.[86] CTime is used to represent an absolute time value. Operations on such a value are very basic and are needed in a multitude of methods, but it would be hard to logically position a time object somewhere in an all-encompassing hierarchical system. The question of what a representation of a specific time should be derived from is hard to answer; this concept is too basic to be inserted into a hierarchy. So, while CTime objects can be integrated into custom-made hierarchies, they themselves are not derived from any superclass: representations of time are solitary objects within the MFC model.

Interface and Implementation

Now that we have a small hierarchy of celestial bodies represented in our object-oriented program design, we still face the task of implementing the actual simulation algorithm. Discussing this algorithm itself is outside the scope of the present work. We are more interested in where such an algorithm would be placed in an object-oriented design. This touches a key question of any object-oriented system, one that we will come back to throughout this work: where and how do processes take place? Do they happen within objects, between objects, or in both places? While Simondon stresses the notion of objects as being through becoming,[87] the concepts of both OOP and OOO define objects qua their relative stability.

In object-oriented ontology, real objects need sensual objects as a bridge between them, leading to a chain of objects. Sensual or real objects cannot touch each other directly. The sensual object acts as an interface between real objects, or the real object as an interface between sensual objects. In object-oriented programming, objects also cannot touch directly: they are broken down into interface and implementation parts. The interface part acts as an—incomplete—directory of methods and variables made available to other objects. It never exposes everything on an object's inside to the outside. It can even announce methods, which at the time of such an announcement are not even fully defined. Only when these methods are being invoked will a real-time decision be made by the software in regards to which version of the method would be appropriate to use in the current situation. So, OOP's interface is on the one hand a sensual object, since it serves as the interface with other objects while not exposing the whole enactability on reality of its real object—which would be the implementation. Methods can execute different code, depending on criteria inaccessible from the outside, allowing for a program to change during runtime without damaging the object's identifiability. The implementation part, on the other hand, represents the real object in the totality of its enactability in the program.

As for the solar system simulation, in object-oriented programming the obvious implementation would be a superclass representing all the components of a solar system needed for its simulation on the level of celestial bodies. An instance of such a solar system class would then have to incorporate member classes for every celestial body in the solar system. But which object would be the one to describe the relations between all the data and methods of the solar system object? One could create methods in the solar system class that would contain the algorithm needed for the simulation, such as modifying a planet's position in space depending on the position and movement of other celestial bodies as time progresses. But the intended way of handling such a simulation is a technique called message-passing.

Objects can send and receive messages. The concept of message-passing allows for messages to be sent to an object, which then decides how to handle the message. This way an object is able to handle requests dynamically, depending on the type of data sent to it. This illustrates how both sides in an object-to-object interaction are involved. This interaction is not a simple sender-receiver relationship, but a rich exchange in which both objects involved do not fully touch each other but are selective with regards to which input to accept at all. An object representing a planet could send a message to other planet objects, informing them about its own location in space. These other planets would then change their position in space accordingly. This way, one could create a very simple simulation of gravity, but none of the objects involved would have any access to other object properties not needed for the calculation of gravitational effects.

Thus, message-passing is not just a concept of inexhaustibility, it is also a concept of indirection. Objects do not exhaust each other, and do not even touch directly, but they do communicate by messages, which can be seen as an implementation of the concept of sensual objects.

Inexhaustibility of Programs

Let us return to the solar system simulation example one last time. We found that the object ontology offered by object-oriented programming languages is a lax one, since there can be objects outside the hierarchy.

The solar system object, the object which hosts our simulation, would need to be instantiated at some point, since it cannot create itself. There has to be code outside the solar system class. Of course, there might be another object, which again incorporates the solar system class (a superclass to the solar system) representing a galaxy. But the Milky Way is not useful for simulating the gravitational effects in our solar system, and this would just move the problem to another level. The object-oriented programming paradigm is an *abstraction* from the hardware the program will eventually be running on, since the central processing unit (CPU) does not "know" objects. The compiler or interpreter program must have done its task of translation to machine code before the CPU can run the program—and after this translation the object concept is lost to the CPU. These translator programs reduce object-orientation to a very basic sequence of memory operations, which the chip can process. This would only change if object-oriented hardware were being built, hardware that would render compilers or interpreters useless—but object-oriented chip designs like the Intel iAPX 432, which was introduced in 1981, eventually failed. They were slow and expensive, and new technologies more suitable to the limitations of hardware prove more efficient—and so the idea of object-orientation in chips has only found very limited application.[88]

Programming languages have come a long way in the last 60 years. They moved from a primitive set of commands in order to directly access a processor's memory to complex semantics, completely abstracted from the hardware its programs will run on. All high-level programming languages need an intermediary between statements made in such a language and the hardware programs are supposed to run on—these intermediaries are either compilers (programs that in a time-consuming way translate high-level programming languages to machine code the processor can work with) or interpreters (which basically fulfill the same task in real-time). In any case, there is a medium between the high-level language and the machine.[89]

While we described objects in object-oriented ontology as broken down into a real and a sensual part (which we superficially likened to the concepts of implementation and interface in programming) we need to understand that the whole relation of the statements made in a high-level programming language to the hardware the written program will run on is the relation of model and reality. The hardware of the chip forms the ultimate reality of the program, since the hardware defines the reality against which the model put on top of it must work. The reality of the hardware again is its context, the wider environment of the machinery, its applications, and the people using it.

The limits of a program's enactability of its reality are in the hardware it runs on and the time available. A self-modifying program could enact an infinite amount of reality given sufficient time. So, the real object is inexhaustible by the relations it enters into with sensual objects. Programs running on a chip can never exhaust it. It is impossible to list all the programs that could be executed on the chip. It is not even possible to know in advance if all these programs will actually come to an end. Alan Turing described this phenomenon, which later became known as the "halting problem": it is undecidable if an arbitrary computer program will eventually finish running or will continue running forever.[90] The halting problem extends inexhaustibility (we cannot know the totality of an object) to the proof of inexhaustibility (it is unintelligible if one can know the totality of an object).

Object-oriented ontology aims at treating all objects equally, which rules out any central perpetrator. In object-oriented programming, it seems that there is no central perpetrator either, with objects acting independently of any central instance. In reality, object-orientation today is a paradigm put on top of hardware, which is incapable of working without a central perpetrator. So, while the language in which the program is modeled is object-oriented, it is important to understand that these objects are constructions in a language, which again tries to mimic things and relations in reality.

Objects act on behalf of themselves as long as one stays at the object's level of abstraction. On the level of the chip these objects are nonexistent— the CPU only acts upon memory, where certain information is stored. The CPU and the operating system will make decisions without the objects "knowing," for example for dispatching: since programs today run mostly on computers with more than one central processing unit, it is necessary to distribute tasks (or object methods) to different CPUs.

The intuition of being surrounded by objects with a certain independence from each other is at the root of both models, OOP and OOO.

But object-oriented ontology rejects the concept of a reducibility of objects to other objects: even though every object can be broken down into its parts (representing new objects): these objects do not exhaust the bigger object they form. There is nothing "below" objects in ooo. oop, however, is a model deliberately put on top of the more primitive and non-intuitive computational concept of memory.

This shows how object-oriented programming is a model working only at a certain level of abstraction, thus constituting the major difference between object-oriented programming and object-oriented ontology: the former being a model applied pragmatically in one domain, the latter aiming for a complete metaphysics.

Recursion and Partial Touch

ooo does not allow for a hierarchy of objects—its ontology is flat. This is seemingly in contradiction to the object hierarchy found in object-oriented programming. But what does ooo's flatness actually mean? Object-oriented ontology holds that the Kantian rift between the human and the thing-in-itself is not exclusive to this particular relation.[91] It holds that there is a rift between all objects; no object can directly and exhaustively "touch" any other object. Thus, there can be no vertical relation in which living conscious beings form a dominant relation with everything else. Does this mean that there cannot be any other kind of object hierarchy as a means of ordering, or better: as a means of identifying objects and how they relate systematically? Even though one of object-oriented programming's most obvious traits is its object hierarchy, this order does not prioritize some objects over others in terms of how these objects interact with or exhaust each other. There are even objects outside the hierarchy (like the CTime object mentioned above). It seems that the idea of non-hierarchical inheritance is suitable for object-oriented ontology: ooo defines objects as independent from their parts and their wider context, but this definition creates the problem of identifiability: a thing so extremely independent is in danger of not being identifiable as a thing at all. There has to be some relation to, some interwovenness with the cosmos surrounding it. A complete non-relation is not thinkable, yet "partial autonomy has yet to be explained,"[92] Harman holds: "The problem is that objects cannot be touched 'in part,' because there is a sense in which objects have no parts."[93] If objects do not have parts which would allow for "partial touch" and objects are independent from their inside and outside, how can ooo account for the relation of essential features of an object to the object itself?

Possibly object-oriented programming's concept of inheritance can be useful here: its hierarchy does not elevate certain objects ontologically—it even allows objects outside the hierarchy, and the only purpose of the hierarchy is in structuring object's self-similarities. This structuring is due to the pragmatic nature of object-oriented programming languages, which aim at making complex realities verbalizable and thus manageable for a (human) software developer. Hierarchies of self-similar objects have proven useful in a number of cases. But as in the example of the solar system simulation above, it is up to the programmer to uncover such hierarchies by observing the reality they[94] want to map into computer memory. And it is not a very useful technique when forced upon structures, which have no self-similar traits. But stochastic (not exact) self-similarity can be observed in objects (or compound objects) from solar systems to fern leaves, from lightings to sea shells, from mountain ranges to coastlines. And self-similarity does not necessarily elevate the human perspective, since it is a fact observable in nature.

It was only in 1975 that Benoît Mandelbrot described objects that are "equally 'rough' at all scales."[95] As opposed to the smooth shapes of classic geometry, fractals have rough edges. In these rough edges the shape of the fractal is repeated. This repetition of shape in theory is not limited, while in nature generally three to five repetitions are observed. Regardless of how close one looks, fractals never get simpler.

Fractals can be created using recursive functions, i.e. functions that call themselves. In the early 20th century, American mathematician Stephen Cole Kleene invented this technique, which is common in informatics nowadays. We want to suggest recursion theory as a starting-point to discuss the problem of partial touch in ooo: how can an object, which always has a wider context to dissolve into and ever-tinier parts to be broken down into, stay identifiable as an object without melting objects again into an *apeiron*-like mass? Harman suggests that an object's sensual qualities can in part be used to identify objects—but this identification becomes problematic when objects form new objects from relations to other objects, and since there is no direct access to the real-object-pole, how can we know that we are not talking about different objects that just have identically appearing sensual poles?

What constitutes an object's independence and what its stability? Recursion theory suggests that an object's relative independence and stability stems from its interwovenness in its wider context and own parts. Objects are recursive as they are defined by their relative position in an endless chain of recursions. An instance of a recursive function stays independent, "unified, like Leibniz's monads,"[96] but is interwoven in its recursion—as a whole, not in part. All objects have a relative position to other objects in the cosmos, and are interwoven in bigger objects. Their interwovenness gives them the partial stability which makes them identifiable as specific objects. If they were not interwoven in such a way they would either be in non-relation, which would make them absolutely unidentifiable, or they would be completely exhaustible, which on the one hand would make them easily identifiable, but on the other would lead to a completely determinist or even halted world. While recursion solves this problem, it asks for a certain self-similarity of objects, which probably is not a necessary condition of objects containing other objects.

A real object is the totality of its enactability on reality, and this must include the object's recursion: an object is always just an entity in an endless line, even though it is an identifiable entity. But a real object is not interwoven in a line, but in a mesh or other kind of structure, which we aim to specify in more detail in chapter 4.

Chapter 3

Interfacing to Haecceity

Preserving Object Legacy

Object-oriented ontology holds that any two objects touching each other ("confronting" in ooo terminology) generate a new object. "Any relation immediately generates a new object."[97] This new object is real and capable of "[withstanding] certain changes in [its] components,"[98] i.e. the objects that formed the new object. Some questions arise due to this definition of object genesis.

Does this formation happen within time? That is, is there a before and after of such an object-formation? If there is not, then all possible object-relations are always already sensually realized, which would contradict the existence of the real object's surplus, the capacity of yet unrealized being. ooo rejects the idea of everything being fully realized at any time, since this notion would not account for emergence (and lead to determinism). This leaves the possibility of object-formation happening within time. Object-formation must therefore be a process, which can be broken down into three phases: the existence of two separate objects, a fusion between them, followed by the existence of a united or merged object. Harman describes fusion and fission as processes within an object, between two object-poles,[99] but we are interested in a fusion of two objects that must have been separate before, since otherwise they could not have been regarded as objects in the first place.

If at some point in time two objects start to fuse, what changed in comparison to the previous situation? Do we find a discrete or a gradual change—or even both? If the change is discrete, then a threshold of sorts would be needed to "decide" whether the fusion would be regarded as having taken place or not (and how such a fusion differs from a mere addition or enhancement, if at all). This leads to the question of the entity that decides upon the truth of a "successful" fusion of two objects.

The key characteristics of objects in object-oriented ontology is that they are in a certain way independent from their wider context and from their inner workings:[100] both can change to a certain extent, yet the object stays "the same." If that certain extent is exceeded, an object does not stay the same, but either forks into more objects or stops existing as an object at all. The problem in this statement is in the terms "to a certain extent" and "the same," because they imply a perspective: who is to define that extent? Who is to judge whether an object stays consistent or breaks apart? These questions seem to lead us away from realism to correlationism, but is this necessarily the case?

In order to elevate objects to be "the chief dramatis personae of philosophy"[101] one must, arguably, be able to identify them as such. While acknowledging that this is to demand an epistemological answer to an ontological question, we want to ask: how can we make sure that objects are not just a mental construction: that what we are doing is not *identifying* objects, but actually *constructing* them according to the possibilities and limits of human epistemic capacity? Is there any reality to these constructions?

In chapter 2 the open/closed principle was introduced, a software development strategy to ensure that even changing objects can continuously be accessed without breaking the context, i.e. the program relying on such an object. The relative stability of objects in object-oriented ontology works similarly: while an object can change on the inside (speaking in terms of computer science: its private methods—those which are not exposed to the object's outside—can change dramatically) its surroundings might not be "aware" of these changes at all. Also, an object's surroundings can change without the object changing in the least. So, when does an object in object-oriented programming actually change from the perspective of its context, i.e. the program using it? It changes when its interface becomes incompatible with the previous version of the object's interface. The computer science's object is generally identified through the totality of its interfaces with the outside. Its internal workings might be unknown, undocumented or even kept secret intentionally, but when the interface changes, we cannot talk about the same object anymore. It is the interface through which the object is being accessed by the program making use of it. So, in oop the extent of change allowed must happen on the object's inside. If change breaks established interfaces, then we must consider the object a new object, incompatible with previous versions.

Another possibility of change is to extend objects with new, additional interfaces. These allow for extending an object's capabilities without breaking established modes of use (its "legacy"). This is common practice, in order to allow for progress while preserving compatibility to programs developed earlier.

The "interface" in object-oriented ontology is the sensual-object-pole, as this is how the object appears to a specific other object, since this appearance is a co-creation with a second real object. Comparing interfaces is the only way to decide whether an object is still the same. But the method is unreliable, since it does not account for—to say it in oop terms—the reality of the object, but only for its sensuality. This unreliability is a key characteristic of ooo, as it reflects an object's ability to change on the inside while staying the same for its context. These hidden internal changes cannot be detected from the outside, which aligns with the concept of an object's relative stability.

These thoughts hint at the problem of extension versus modification. If an object were merely extended—that is, enhanced by certain additional sensual qualities—but the object can still be confronted in the same way, we should not regard such a change as "breaking the object's legacy." Thus, we could speak of the same object. If for example the European Union decided to enter into a trade agreement with China, this would extend the interfaces of the European Union, but would still allow existing interfaces continued operation. But when the United Kingdom leaves the European Union, an existing interface would break: namely, that of all the non-EU countries doing business with the UK, a country that would then not be an EU member state anymore. Would the EU still be called the EU? Of course it would. Would the UK be still called the UK? Definitely. So, in the strict sense of informatics, the loss of the UK would break legacy code (i.e. agreements, expectations, politics) but in the sense of object-oriented ontology, both objects UK and EU would continue to exist. Why? What is the difference?

Even though the EU can lose an important part, it would still be the EU. Even if the EU's name were changed to "European Mainland Union" or some other odd moniker, it would be obvious that this organization is the successor to the EU. So, there is a link to the past, a sense of legacy that constitutes an object's stability. An object's stability is not in its name or in the sum of its parts, since both of these can change dramatically. We want to hold—temporarily, until chapter 5—that an object's stability can be found in its traceability through time. It is necessary to know an object's legacy in order to be able to identify it as an object at all.[102]

But how about objects that can be traced through time, but change fundamentally nevertheless? How about today's reunified Germany and the fascist Germany of 1933 to 1945? Most people would argue that today's Germany is completely different and cannot be compared to the Germany of the National Socialist era. But it is precisely statements like these that prove the traceability of the object "Germany" through time: by stating that today's state is vastly different from its earlier incarnation, it shows the relation, the need of historic demarcation. One would not state that one cannot compare today's Germany to the Antarctica of 1933 to 1945; this would be just an arbitrary statement. So, objects stay the same if they can be traced through time, even when their sensual object or sensual-qualities-pole changes. Consequentially, today's Federal Republic of Germany (*Bundesrepublik Deutschland*) is regarded as the same international legal personality as the German Reich (*Deutsches Reich*). As Jocelyn Benoist notes, it is not geographic or other facts that make an object, but what we mean by it when we talk about it, and how we define it.[103] What "we" mean by it is the result of a common way of identifying objects. But ooo now extends the rift beyond the human-world relation in order to allow for confrontation, and thus identification between all kinds of entities. The identification of an object is in the sensual relation we have with it and thus it is specific to the other object in this relation (in this case, human epistemic capacity). The same object will appear differently to different subjects, but as long as there is any traceability through time for a certain number of subjects regarding what they mean by it and how they define it as the subjects, it will be regarded the same object. However, these relations are not limited to subject-object relations, but can occur between any set of objects bound to other objects by a common reality—a relation that can hardly be capable of producing "meaning" as long as it is defined as the relation between intension (the properties of the thing referred to as necessary to identify it) and extension (which is the actual thing to which the term refers to).

Temporal Distance—Gadamer

When we identify a thing as a certain object, whether categorical or concrete, fictional or physical, a hermeneutic process takes place, i.e. a production of understanding. Gadamer's analysis of hermeneutics focuses on the role of time for understanding. He rejects historical objectivism, but his hermeneutics are far from being constructivist (he does not shy away from terms like the "correct understanding"[104] of a text). Gadamer acknowledges the tradition in which we are embedded when entering into a hermeneutic process, but his analysis does not lead to postmodernist epistemic arbitrariness. In *Truth and Method*, Gadamer focuses on texts and other cultural artifacts, but his analysis can also be read as a realist theory of identification, as it creates awareness of the pitfalls of the process such as the tendency to only identify things as objects that have certain traits one already knows and therefore expects from them. He holds that the process of construal is itself already governed by an expectation of meaning that follows from the context of what has happened before.[105] Gadamer is well aware of the subjectivity of this process. Thus, while we use the term identification, his own interest is in the more complex process of interpretation:

> The prejudices and fore-meanings that occupy the
> interpreter's consciousness are not at his free disposal. He
> cannot separate in advance the productive prejudices that
> enable understanding from the prejudices that hinder it and

lead to misunderstandings. Rather, this separation must
take place in the process of understanding itself, and hence
hermeneutics must ask how that happens. But that means it
must foreground what has remained entirely peripheral in
previous hermeneutics: temporal distance and its significance
for understanding.[106]

Temporal distance is key for "correct understanding" and, we would
argue also for the identifiability of objects: when we identify an object,
we assume and expect a "unity of meaning,"[107] an entity that can be
differentiated from its surroundings. Gadamer calls this expectation that
guides all understanding a "fore-conception of completeness" ("Vorgriff
der Vollkommenheit"), which is always determined by the specific content.
Not only does the reader assume an immanent unity of meaning, but their
understanding is likewise guided by the constant transcendent expectations
of meaning that proceed from the relation to the truth of what is being
said."[108] If applied not just to cultural artifacts, but to natural objects like
the sun or the moon, it becomes clear that by assuming an immanent unity
of meaning we lay the grounds for something to become an object—for us.
But meaning is as endangered as it is dangerous: it slices an inexhaustible
real into palpable pieces. When regarding meaning as the relation between
intension (the qualities necessary to make something a specific object) and
extension (the sum of all objects having such properties), we can observe the
following: Gadamer describes how only in retrospect do we know what we
did not know before, and the fact that we did not know it before. Meaning
can therefore be understood as a fabric of relations woven retroactively. We
are naming a set of qualities in a certain way, and therefore make something
identifiable as an object: we create sensual objects in language, and since
there cannot be a sensual-object-pole without a corresponding real object,
we do create a part of ourselves by establishing terms. These terms again
shape our fore-conception of completeness. It is terms, or concepts, which
shape our capability of coming up with more concepts. By collapsing a
multitude of objects into one broad concept (like "women," "men," "the
people" or "the establishment") we do not just overmine, but deliberately
fall short of the wealth and variety of objects we have already gathered. This
leads to fore-conceptions of completeness that are not just less saturated and

overly broad and simplistic, but have been shown to eventually cause terror and tremendous suffering.

In both Gadamer's hermeneutics and Harman's ooo, time plays an important role when it comes to identifying objects as such. By observing the sun or the moon over time we can trace their movements, their existence through time, and thus we get a sense of their relative stability. We can also make predictions about their future movements, since we expect them to behave in a predictable way.

Interestingly enough, our expectations for fictional objects are much higher than towards everyday objects such as a regular workweek. A workweek fulfills the criteria of an object, but an immanent unity of meaning might be hard to find in it. However, a novel or a movie as a thoughtfully constructed dramatic work of art exceptionally raises our expectations of such a unity of meaning. The more constructed an object (the less random or arbitrary), the more easily it can satisfy the fore-conception of completeness. Surrounded by a world of arbitrary, hard-to-understand or even nonsensical events, cultural artifacts are bound to deliver unities of meaning.[109] Creating these unities of meanings is, according to Konrad Fiedler, the work of the artist: striving to express—to make visible—a stable knowledge about the appearance of the world.[110]

Unities of meaning, as relations between intension and extension, are a necessary prerequisite for object identification; there is no such thing as a meaningless object. An object might not serve a specific purpose, but as long as it is independent enough from its surroundings to be identifiable, it has,—or better, *is*—an immanent unity of meaning. Objects can be fictional, but they cannot be arbitrary or change in any arbitrary fashion without losing their "thisness": the relative stability of objects could therefore also be called relative identifiability.

Thus, if meaning precedes identification, it is a stability that precedes identification. Stability, however, cannot be identified as such if not observed over time. Stability makes objects traceable through time, making time a necessary prerequisite for the finding of meaning that we are looking for in objects to identify them as objects. But as we will continue to see, time (and space) are not the media of confrontation, but the very consequence of the tension between intension and extension, the consequence of what Gadamer calls meaning:

> [Time and space] are the tension of identity-in-difference, the strife between real objects and their accidents (space) or intentional objects[111] and their accidents (time). And since under this model both space and time involve accidents as one of their poles, in a sense it is true that both are forms of perception, and Kant was right to say so—though only in a Kantianism extended beyond humans to flowers and inanimate things.[112]

Temporal distance for Gadamer is necessary for social processes, which generate "common meaning," as he calls it. "The task of hermeneutics is to clarify this miracle of understanding, which is not a mysterious communion of souls, but sharing in a common meaning."[113] But how can a realist, non-anthropocentric philosophy like ooo depend on social processes as a necessity for object identification? Do we start to wrap object-orientation into a correlationist philosophy? Do we run the risk of overmining? Denying objects an existence on their own appears to be an overmining process. But that is not the goal of this operation. It is not necessary to reduce objects to their relations, but it is necessary to relate to objects to identify them as such. The relative stability that object-oriented ontology ascribes to objects first needs to be "discovered" by a process of ontological hermeneutics, which doesn't stop at texts, but covers all of the world's phenomena. And during such a hermeneutic process, the shapes of objects become clearer—or they lead to the destruction of objects that cannot or can no longer contain themselves.

One must therefore differentiate between the human capacity to identify objects through hermeneutic processes, and the temptation to deduce ontological superiority from this capacity. The history of philosophy has come up with tools and methods like phenomenology that try to remove human subjectivity from its observations, but ultimately this is impossible, if for no other reason than the limitations of human enactability on time. This however does not mean that there is no reality beyond human epistemic capacity—and neither does it mean that there is no access to any reality outside the human mind. The challenge lies in making sure that what we identify as objects qualifies for that status (which is relatively easy) and that we develop the tools to identify objects without limiting them to adhering or conforming to our expectations (much more difficult). In any case, we run the risk of only identifying objects that are just variations of what we already know.[114]

The hermeneutics of object-oriented ontology make change digestible: the radically new, accounted for in the real object's surplus, is dragged into the realm of the sensual by hermeneutic operations under the inevitable impression of tradition: "Working out of the hermeneutical situation means the achievement of the right horizon of inquiry for the questions evoked by the encounter with tradition."[115] Tradition here is just another term for the ability to trace an object through time.

Identification and Change—Putnam and Kripke

Gadamer's "correct understanding" does not refer to the generation of meaning in the speaker's mind alone. Rather, meaning is generated in social processes within time. In the traditional (pre-Putnam) linguistic theory, which came forth using Aristotelian logic, "meaning" is a term under tension between the poles of intension and extension, the reference. And while in the traditional theory two terms can have different intensions and refer to the same extension, two terms cannot differ in extension and yet have the same intension. Putnam holds that the traditional theory refers to knowing a meaning (intensionally) simply as being in a certain ("narrow") psychological state. The theory also holds that the meaning of a term determines its extension, and the same intension always refers to the same extension.

Putnam refuses the theory of the same intension always referring to the same extension by bringing forth his famous Twin-Earth thought experiment: on a distant planet, very similar to earth, water is not made up from H_2O, but from XYZ. Putnam also assumes that we're in the year 1750 and therefore chemical knowledge about the composition of water molecules would still need another 50 years to be discovered—on both earths. Putnam further assumes the existence of Oscar1, an earth-inhabitant, and his perfect clone, Oscar2, living on Twin-Earth. Both think about "water," so they are in the same narrow psychological state, but they do not think about the same thing. The intensions of both Oscar1 and Oscar2 are the same; their respective extensions however differ (H_2O on earth and XYZ on Twin-Earth), if only on a chemical level. In Putnam's thought experiment, H_2O and XYZ when observed by non-chemists appear identical. There is a difference on the molecular level that people were oblivious about in 1750. So, what both Oscars think of is the same in their head, since they do not yet know anything about the molecular structure of what they both call water. In any case, he holds that "internalism is refuted."[116] As he puts it: "According to the externalist, the mind necessarily involves the world; what one means and thinks is partly constituted by what there is in the world. Putnam's famous slogan is 'cut the pie any way you like, meanings just ain't in the head'."[117] Putnam's conclusions are scientistic in the sense that in his thought-experiments science delivers the only authoritative worldview: it is chemists who have the final say on what water "really" is. Speaking in terms of object-oriented ontology, water as its chemical composition, be it H_2O or XYZ, is not any more real than the everyday object we drink or swim in.

So, what does Putnam's thought experiment prove? The meaning of "water" is not determined entirely by the psychological states of people thinking (about) it: two different persons can have the same intensions referring to different extensions. But it also means that it is necessary to know what something is in order to refer to it, a notion Kripke rejects. His main contention against Putnam is that it is not necessary at all to know the truth about anything in order to refer to it. For Kripke it is irrelevant if "what is in the head" refers to an outside reality, which is sufficiently known and true: reference is rather determined by a "chain of communication," a succession of social acts or processes, about which the thinker is most likely oblivious.[118] For Kripke, names are rigid designators:

> A singular term 'X' is a rigid designator if and only if 'X might not have been X' and 'someone/thing other than X might have been X' are unambiguously false. By this test typical proper names are plainly rigid designators but most definite descriptions are not. So are natural kind terms (like 'gold', 'water', and 'the tiger', which can replace 'X' grammatically in the test sentences) but not (most) descriptions of natural kinds

(like 'the world's most precious metal', 'the most dangerous
kind of creature on the planet').[119]

Coming back to the Danziger Straße example from chapter 1, we can
now safely say with Kripke that referring means tapping a vast shared
historical residue. While Danziger Straße in East Berlin has changed its
name multiple times, it stays the same object because it can be traced
through time. The object's legacy—or as Kripke put it, the "chain of
communication" that lead to its identifiability—is intact. This shared
historical residue can be subsumed as an object's qualities "to identify it
from the outside."[120] Kripke helps with identifying an object while not caring
if what we refer to really exists or is true; Gadamer, however, focuses on the
object's meaning. This difference is crucial, as by identifying objects we do
not just reference them. Referencing requires pre-existing shared knowledge,
but for the process of identifying, such pre-existing (shared) knowledge
might even be considered a hindrance: it is after all the source of the fore-
conception of completeness. The chain of communication ties one to the
tradition and makes it hard to identify objects outside of it.

Familiarity and Strangeness, Identification and Allure

We should differentiate more precisely between referencing/referring to
and identifying objects. Identifying in the common sense always means
"re-cognizing" something: identification is matching perception against
preconceived patterns. Just as a criminal's fingerprints can only be identified
by matching those found at the crime scene to the ones already stored in
a police database, identification always means going back to information
previously collected, comparing and matching something against it. The
Latin origin of referring makes this process obvious, since "referre" means
carrying back. A mere carrying back, however, cannot identify new objects.
The risk of just finding what is already known, or slight variations of it, is
high. This is a classic problem in the history of philosophy. Meno's Paradox
hints at the problem of searching for something one does not yet know.
Harman, however, suggests that by means of "allure" it is possible to go
beyond what is known—a strategy pursued by artists rather than scientists.
Allure "is the separation of an object from its qualities."[121] It is "the principle

of revolution as such, since only allure makes quantum leaps from one state of reality into the next by generating a new relation between objects."[122] So instead of identifying new objects, object-oriented ontology focuses on a strange recombination of objects, where an object is separated from its qualities in order to enter into new relations. It does not search for radically new objects, but for recombinations of existing objects or their qualities. "Allusion and allure are legitimate forms of knowledge,"[123] Harman holds. This "revolutionary" knowledge comes forth by the genesis of new relations—a change from the known to the yet unknown. This change is, at least for the human mind, hermeneutic work:

> Hermeneutic work is based on a polarity of familiarity
> and strangeness; but this polarity is not to be regarded
> psychologically... as the range that covers the mystery of
> individuality, but truly hermeneutically—i.e., in regard to what
> has been said: the language in which the text addresses us, the
> story that it tells us. Here too there is a tension. It is in the play
> between the traditionary text's strangeness and familiarity to
> us, between being a historically intended, distanced object and
> belonging to a tradition. The true locus of hermeneutics is this
> in-between.[124]

This in-between, this interplay of strangeness and familiarity, is characteristic of the phenomenon of allure. What Gadamer calls the "true locus of hermeneutics" is—extended beyond mind-text relations—what allure is between objects and their qualities: it is where a new, identifiable object comes into existence. But while Gadamer's interest lies solely in the relation between reader and text, we must assume a hermeneutic locus in relations between all objects, a necessity for the flat object-oriented ontology.

We are back at the ontological problem of objects being "the chief dramatis personae of [a realist object-oriented] philosophy,"[125] but being in need of social processes to identify them as such. The realist position would be to assume that objects exist without being identified. But what is it that exists without being identified? If we need sensual-object-poles to identify objects, how can we talk about objects without having identified any of them outside the scope of our perception? How can we justify the leap of faith that objects beyond our perception behave like those within the realm of our perception? Objects within the range of our perception already behave in strange ways: they are already inexhaustible to us and their behavior is predictable only under very well defined conditions. We do not need to differentiate between objects on this and the other side of the doors of perception. Also, social processes as means to refer to objects are suspicious, because they seemingly challenge the realist position that objects have existed before, will continue to exist after, and currently exist beyond human cognition. Since object-orientation allows for any object to "perceive," i.e. "confront" any other object, the ontological superiority of the human is not necessary for objects to be "perceived." In ooo, Berkeley's anti-realist "to be is to be perceived" is somehow being re-imagined as "perception" by any kind of object. This epistemic process, which Harman moves to an abstract level so that it can take place between any kind of object, seems like a way out: any kind of sensual-object-pole relates to its real-object-pole (and vice versa). This "sincerity"[126] of the "experience" within an object is a discrete concept: "The only thing that can be done to sincerity is simply to end it."[127] In ooo real and sensual-object-poles either touch or they do not— their relation is "sincere" or it is not at all. Harman acknowledges that the touching of real objects with other real objects "occurs neither directly nor through any short-distance mediation. It must occur in some much more mediated or complicated manner."[128] How would such a touching happen? Since real objects cannot touch without a sensual object in between, there is a distance between two real objects, as there is between two sensual objects.[129] But since in object-oriented ontology any object contains a sensual-object-pole, even a cold rock, is there ever a situation in which two objects cannot touch, not even by the most remote distance or mediated by any yet unidentified cosmic force? Can objects stay unidentified somewhere in the cosmos, in the realm of ideas, or anywhere at all? If there existed something unidentified it would certainly not be an object, as an object must be identified as such (or at least be identifiable) regardless of the identifying object's nature. An object cannot be regarded as an object in the absence of confrontation.

Roy Bhaskar claims that the idea of existence being exclusive to experienceable entities is wrong. Such "ontological monovalence" would mean the impossibility of change, according to Bhaskar.[130] If absence were to be in the reality of an object that has not yet entered into a relation with another object, we would get into a paradoxical situation, as what has not entered into any relation cannot be called an object at all. If absence however is necessary for change but cannot be accounted for outside of objects (within object-oriented ontology), absence must be realized within the real-object-poles of objects, which have not yet enacted their common reality to give birth to a new object. Thus, a recombination of qualities in different objects merges them "revolutionarily" to generate new objects. The absence of relations must play a crucial role for an object's identity. In contrast to general structuralist thinking, an object is not just what it is not, but *also* is what it is not.

Chapter 4

Genesis and Integration

The Unsigned Agreement—On the Necessity of Non-Relations

In chapter 3 it was found that object identification poses a special problem in ooo. In the following we want to touch on ooo's open questions in the highly-intertwined fields of the genesis, identification, and integration of objects. These issues form a circle of interdependence, and the ability to explain how they relate seems to be helpful for any philosophy aiming to grant objects ontological priority.

First, it is necessary for objects to be identifiable, because their identifiability is what separates them from worlds of floating qualities, devoid of stable or independent objects, as described in the theory of the *apeiron* or other philosophies of the "pre-individual," which are explicitly rejected by ooo. Second, it is necessary for objects to be generatable, because generatability is a prerequisite for change, for emergence. If objects were ungeneratable, one would need to hold that there is no emergence, which means that either there are no objects at all or that all objects have always already existed; both outcomes would be similarly unsuitable for any object-oriented philosophy. Third, it is necessary for objects to be integrable, as only objects that can touch other objects can be identified as objects at all. Integrability thus means the ability to take part in a system established by shared interfaces. A system in this sense is thought of not as a pre-object structure in which objects subsequently fall into place, but as a retroactively formed structure, informed implicitly by the interfaces that objects expose to the outside. Only by exposing certain interfaces it is possible for objects to touch. But as in object-oriented programming, exposed interfaces are only the tip of the iceberg—an object is much deeper than what it exposes to other objects. Integrability therefore means interfaceability, which eventually is a prerequisite for identifiability, where the circle of interdependence of these three necessities closes. Objects need interfaces to identify other objects as such—and to do so, objects needs to provide compatible interfaces. To identify does not mean to exhaust an object, but to connect reliably to the same object over and over again: sameness here referring to a certain stability in its interfaces, not its interior life.

Following up on the European Union example used earlier, we want to go back to the year 1952, when the seed for the EU was planted and look at the generation of this large compound object. In that year Germany, France, Italy, Luxembourg, and the Netherlands formed the European Coal and Steel Community (ECSC), a free trade area and political union for the member states' coal industry. The *Montanunion*, as it was also called, was the world's first supra-national organization, the nucleus of the EU to come. The member states obviously gave birth to a new compound object. It goes without saying that this new community stopped neither Germany nor France nor the other member states from existing. So, while a new object came into being, its parts kept most of their independence. A new object emerged, but its constituents stayed somewhat independent. Explaining the ECSC by reducing it to its nation state components would miss the point of the union. Some (but not all) qualities of the ECSC were in the agreement into which all participating countries entered. The ECSC became a stable set of non-undermining relations, irreducible to its components. But it existed not just in its relations, because the relations themselves changed its relata: namely, by aligning economic and therefore political interests of the two former enemies Germany and France and the other founding members. This was the done with the ultimate goal of preventing European countries from ever going to war with each other again. In having actual effects on its member states, the union formed a non-overmining relation. The ECSC shows how the compound is more than its parts. If we reduced the compound to its components, we would leave out a crucial part, namely its relations. But it is too simple to read the agreement solely as a relation, since the agreement the member states entered into is also an additional object that relates to all member states. Since a transnational treaty is not part of any nation alone, it constitutes a new object, which is necessary for the compound object of the ECSC to exist at all. It is the part that allows for the whole.

The relations of the agreement with nation states, however, do not necessarily have to be legally binding relations. They could also be hypothetical relations, a potential for something to happen, an offer to other European nation states, while remaining an unsigned agreement for the time being. But it would be wrong to call such an unsigned agreement a mere piece of paper without consequences. Its sheer existence, and the way it non-relates to non-members of the union, can form a new and problematic relation in itself. One might think of the decades of the EU-Turkish relationship basically circling around the fact of Turkey not being part of the European Union. So, any agreement relates to the party drafting it—even if the document is never signed. The agreement must be drafted in a language that all relevant parties understand (i.e. the parties have to be able to generate a shared object to reduce misunderstandings to a minimum). Like many agreements do, it might contain woolly phrasing in order to conceal points on which definite consent will not be reached, but this apparent weakness serves a purpose—even deliberate misunderstandings are contingent on common interfaces. The agreement, signed or unsigned, has to provide a common interface; otherwise, there is no chance of establishing a stable relation. One does not have to sign it in order to relate to it in non-relation. Even negative relation (for example, by rejection or ignorance) is a relation in the way that it is possible to relate to it. In order to relate to it, one needs to share an interface with it, even if one does not actively make use of such an interface. So, we agree with ooo's stance that objects do not need to do anything. But it is necessary for an object to be relatable, even if it is in the most distant, distorting or inconsequential way. The unsigned agreement thus serves as a metaphor for the necessity of relatability at all.

The unsigned agreement reveals that while objects are more than relations, relations are objects, but so are non-relations. By non-relations we mean relations that have not formed new objects, but which in their not doing so still facilitate an object's stability. This is because an object is defined by the interfaces it provides, not by the interfaces it actively uses at a specific moment in time (as opposed to actor-network theory's actants, which are only defined by what they do and by their effects). We do not hold that relations and non-relations are of the same caliber. As Harman notes, there are different degrees of "importance" in object relations.[131] However, with respect to Bhaskar's warning against ontological monovalence, we hold that even an apparent non-relation is a kind of relation in its possibility of a (deeper) relation. This possibility must always be given as long as we give objects ontological priority. The touching of objects, any kind of object genesis, and thus any causation at all is contingent on common interfaces. Everything being able to enter into any kind of relation, be it physically, mentally or in any other way must be equipped with some shared common interface. Everything not exposing such a common interface necessarily establishes another plane of reality, a parallel universe completely concealed from us. This is not Heideggerian concealment on a thing's inside. Objects not exposing common interfaces to at least one other object on the same plane of reality are completely inaccessible, in a way that makes them non-existent on that plane. We must conclude that as long as objects are to be the ontological basis, relatability is necessary: an integration of all objects. Sharing interfaces is what makes all objects "belong to the same plane of reality."[132] Common interfaces are the fabric of integration. And while the idea of a "fabric" of objects is not new, the integration term we propose covers all being, i.e. all objects in ooo's sense, not just sentient beings as in Timothy Morton's "mesh."[133] And this term must not lead us to think of "everything being one" in the way that being is made up of an indeterminate, gradual flow from which consciousness arbitrarily carves out items and labels them objects. Harman would reject such a notion as overmining since it suggests an upward reduction of objects to their relations. Not all objects relate to all other objects at all times, but we hold that all objects must eventually be *relatable*.[134] The actual relations of objects might be strong or weak, but the entity to which relation is impossible is not an entity at all.

Obviously, relatability is actualized in the sensual-object-pole, which is generated in a confrontation of real objects. But the question remains: if all the relations any object can enter into are in the realm of the sensual, how can we talk about a concrete object beyond this relation?

Expectation Management—Is Identifiability a Mere Methodological Problem?

The heart of object-oriented ontology is invisible. Since object-oriented ontology is flat, it treats the most mundane thing such as a plastic bottle as an object in its own right. But as opposed to actor-network-theory, which defines an object as what it (observably) does, but also as opposed to other reductionist theories claiming that things are not ontologically important if they can be reduced to something else (smaller or bigger), ooo's definition requires objects to have an inaccessible, invisible essence. ooo's definition of essence is complicated: the intuition that an object's essence would be identical to its real-object-pole is not correct. An object's essence is in the *tension* between its real-object-pole and its real-qualities-pole. It is in this tension that ooo places all causation, which means "to generate a new relation, and to do this is to create a new object. … The primary meaning of 'cause' is to create a new object."[135] So, an object's essence in ooo is in the relation between its stable real core and its real accidents, but neither of these components is directly accessible. How can we identify an object if its "thisness" lies in a relation between two inaccessible poles? We need to take another leap.

An object's real-qualities-pole is not just connected to its real-object-pole, but also to its sensual-object-pole, a tension that ooo deems an object's eidos, a term used in the Husserlian sense of the necessary phenomena emanating from an object. These phenomena need to be distinguished from unnecessary accidents, which can change without essentially changing the underlying object. Necessity is a prerequisite for the possibility of identification, and in this case the eidos serves as an object's identifier. But while in Husserlian identification phenomena and essence are one, in ooo this identifier relates only indirectly to the real object. An object cannot be reduced to its eidos and an object's eidos cannot be used to reliably relate to its essence.

So, while an object's essence is a tension between two inaccessible entities, its identifier is the tension between an object's inaccessible qualities and its sensual-object-pole. The sensual-object-pole (so) however is not just an interface between the real-qualities-pole (RQ) and the sensual-qualities-pole (SQ), as shown in Harman's fourfold diagrams.[136] A sensual object forms when two real objects touch, so there can never be a sensual object without two real objects confronting each other through it. A sensual object is always both under the influence of and the product of two real objects. And while OOO holds that all relations between objects are distorted in the sense that they do not allow for direct access to the real object, OOO cannot sufficiently explain qualitative differences in grades of distortion, since the real object stays inaccessible. In other words: epistemologically speaking, how can we know we are relating to the same object if distortions vary greatly?

Since one end of the SO-RQ relation is inaccessible and fleeting, an object's identifiability is eventually contingent on its real qualities not losing the relation to their real-object-pole. Stability of essence must prevail, since otherwise this intricate mesh of object relations would be torn apart; since objects are granted priority over processes in OOO, this destabilization should be thought of as an exception, as Harman notes in *Immaterialism*.[137] But even if this local fabric proves to be stable, there is much room for distorting the relation between the real qualities and the sensual-object-pole, an inevitable distortion as OOO holds.[138]

The shortest line between a real object and any way of accessing it is via two tensions. We need to take two leaps since we can only ever touch an object's sensual instantiation.[139] The real-object-pole again "contains" a surplus above and beyond its sensual manifestations, being the totality of its enactability in reality. This surplus on the one hand is inexhaustible, since the relations between objects are inexhaustible and the inaccessible real object is the source of this inexhaustibility. On the other hand, objects must differ from one another; they must be identifiable (which was defined as being traceable through time by providing stable interfaces).

Harman holds that the problem of identifiability of objects is a mere methodological one, since "the difficulty of identifying an object is [OOO's] whole point."[140] OOO refers to the phenomenological method as a tool to bring us closer to a sensual object. In applying this method, through a series of movements of the mind, one strips away accidents from an object and therefore presupposes the existence of a specific sensual object beneath these fleeting qualities. But one can only reduce an object to its eidos if one already knows what to reduce it to. ooo allows us to scrape off the moss covering a statue, which only works because we "know" the statue we can expect underneath. We "know" where to stop, "we" being the sensual object produced from the reality of the statue and the reality of the perceiver's perceptive apparatus. Since we defined identifying as comparing something with data gathered earlier, identification is always informed by expectation. The expectation changes the genesis of the sensual object in a way ranging from identifying a completely different sensual object to not identifying any object at all. But this is the fate of the sensual object-pole, which is always entangled in a co-creational momentum: one could be carving the rock again and again, never to find the statue, because any state of carving is as good as the other. There is a statue and no statue in all phases of the process. ooo acknowledges the distortion taking place between objects and the problems in identifying an object as such is everything but another source of distortion.

All methods of producing, structuring, and storing retrievable data distort the data stored and this distortion affects the ability to identify objects. ooo acknowledges this distortion, but it somehow implies that one can distinguish the object and its distorted qualities phenomenologically. Additionally, a distortion that lets an object be an object for some other objects but not for all others seems to pose a problem for ooo. Objects are being distorted, but they can never be distorted to the point that they become objects and non-objects at the same time. And what is an object to me might not be one for some other confronting entity, and vice versa. A distortion is always a distortion *of an object*. To identify a distortion therefore always includes identifying the underlying object.

The problem here is in the use of the term "object." If a specific relation real a–real b brings forth an object it is a sensual object (a–b), if a relation real a–real c fails and does not bring forth a relation (a–c), ooo would hold that this failure does not affect the reality of both real objects a and c. We conclude from this that relating one real object to another successfully via one sensual object guarantees the existence of such a real object. The "failed" real a–real c relation, however, must be regarded as a relation as well, as was shown before. The failure to relate (i.e. form an object that is somewhat independent of its parts and context) constitutes a relation of non-relation. The object we would like to name "non-object," which comes forth from the non-relation of the real a–real c relation, gains its stability not from the quality of its relations but from the known character of its relata. In other words: by it being known which objects *do not* form a new object, a relation of these known objects is being generated, and therefore a new but non-identifiable object, the non-object, comes into existence.

The questions arise if (1) the real-object-pole holds the totality of an object's enactability on reality, if (2) any relation a real-object-pole can enter into is only possible by means of sensual objects as interfaces, being generated by the touching of two real objects. But since this touching is always distorted and never exhaustive, (3) how can we know that there is more than one real object at all? The problem lies in the impossibility of the identification of the real. We can only identify the object's identity, the object's eidos (in the ooo meaning of the term) insofar as it appears in its corresponding sensual objects, while its essence is a relation beyond any direct access. So, in varying the question above we may ask: how can we make the point that what we allude to is a stable, independent object? The answer is most likely in the *we*, as was suggested by Gadamer, but it is a *we* that should be extended to object-object relations.

A fundamental characteristic of object-oriented ontology lies in the way it treats objects as concrete and mysterious at the same time. ooo is very concrete regarding the borders of objects ontologically, and strongly rejects any epistemic "overmining," which would only let objects dissolve in a network of relations and make them lose their ontological priority. ooo, however, is very mysterious when it comes to objects' capabilities: the relation between the sensual and real-object-poles is inexhaustible, and their real poles are not for other objects to grasp directly.

Real objects in ooo must be (relatively) stable, and the only way to account for such stability is by means of sensual objects. But as real objects are inaccessible and a repository of inexhaustibility, they are ooo's wildcard. Since they hold an inestimable surplus, how can objects, which conceal themselves and are limitless in their ability to relate to sensual objects, be separate and unique entities?[141] How can there be haecceity in something this vague?

Two Dimensions of Integration and the Pan-Object

A real object's relative stability manifests itself only through confrontation with another real object, which is only possible vicariously through the interface of a sensual object. Until a sensual object establishes this connection, a real object is unidentifiable. As long as real objects do not touch, there is no way of sensually telling them apart. This leads to a paradoxical necessity: the only way to grant objects independence is by acknowledging their integration into a fabric of neighboring objects. This integration can be theorized in (at least) two different dimensions: the dimension of object fourfolds connecting on the same level, which we would want to call *horizontal integration*, and the interconnectedness as of objects as being parts of compound objects, which we would want to call *vertical integration*. The Simondon scholar Muriel Combes sums up these two dimensions of integration: "In dephasing, being always simultaneously gives birth to an individual mediating two orders of magnitude [vertical integration] *and* to a milieu at the same level of being [horizontal integration]."[142] ooo regards the interaction between objects not primarily as an effect of one object on another, but as "merely a retroactive effect of a joint object that unites the two, or once did so."[143] So, when two objects relate they are parts of another bigger object (and to fend off any accusation of overmining, one would hold that objects are part of compound objects, but can not be reduced to them). Since we have shown before that all objects on the same plane of reality have to be relatable, this must mean that all objects are always already "merely a retroactive effect" of an object uniting all objects.[144] By introducing such an object we do not want to suggest that the real is always already realized: such an object is no overmining tool, since it is infinite, but not complete.[145]

Contemporary scholar Penas López summarizes Simondon's notion of compatibilization as "a process of individuation [beginning] when communication between ... different orders of magnitude is established."[146] This co-existence of objects on different orders of magnitude and the necessity of interfaceability between all objects leads to the question of the validity of an all-encompassing "world" object, a pan-object containing all objects in the world, physical, mental, more or less real. While Markus Gabriel's realism would flat-out deny the existence of such an object, the case in ooo requires further investigation. The first question is of course: why would the existence of such an object be a problem in the first place? The reason is in the way this deduction seemingly threatens objects' ontological priority. If it were valid within ooo to assume an object containing all objects, then all inter-object relations were just retroactive effects of this pan-object. Objects retroactively containing other objects force the question upon us if any entity could be reduced to the pan-object. If object relations are constituted by a larger object encompassing its component objects, doesn't this establish a priority of the encompassing object? And how would such an object differ from Anaximander's *apeiron* or Simondon's pre-individual?

We want to posit the pan-object as compatible with ooo's fourfold model, given these preliminary considerations: if the pan-object consists of an inaccessible real-object-pole and a sensual-object-pole, which is the other real object to which this sensual object would connect? If we fail to answer this question, the pan-object would become an absurd entity, as it would have to interface with another object to bring forth a sensual object. In doing so it would cease to be an all-encompassing object. Even an all-encompassing object would need another object to touch. There is one way out, however: the object relates to itself. ooo uses the name "sincerity" for a direct relation between the so and ro poles: "Sincerity is just another name for an object existing as what it is and nothing else."[147] The pan-object would therefore be the totality of reality and thus the only object to exist in a state of constant sincerity, for it has no other object to appear distorted to. So, while all the objects the pan-object encompasses can appear to each other, and *will appear distorted* to each other, on the scale of the pan-object this is just a tempest in a teacup.

The pan-object seemingly contradicts Harman's position that "no final, encompassing object that could be called a universe" can exist.[148] But this would only be the case in a universe that does not contain "dormant" objects, as Harman calls real objects, which at a certain point do not relate to other objects at all. The notion of the dormant object is being rejected here as long as it designates an object not providing any interfaces, meaning not being open for any kind of (future) relation. We hold it to be necessary that an object is always in a state of relatability, offering interfaces, even if there is no "active" connection at any given moment. If dormant objects were to be understood as completely disconnected and unconnectable entities, then they would be indistinguishable from Simondon's pre-individual, which Harman rejects (we will look into Simondon and Harman's rejection of his position in chapter 4). If dormant objects were just temporarily in a mode of being where they do not "perceive,"[149] as Harman holds in *The Quadruple Object*, we have to consider the bidirectionality of any relation: while "even inanimate objects do not react to all the data available to them,"[150] this "dormant" quality does not cut off the possibility or even necessity of being perceived (in the broadest sense of the term as applied to objects in ooo). This necessity is what we mean by providing interfaces, which relate object fourfolds and form the pan-object.

The sincerity in which the pan-object appears to itself is in line with Harman's early definition as "an adhesive: a powerful glue cementing subject and object to such an extent that they no longer appear separable."[151] Even though every object needs an opposite object as a mediator, the totality of all objects does not have one. It *cannot* have one: the pan-object, which does appear undistorted to itself, is the reason why we can have realism at all. The contact with itself is a prime example of sincerity: "the only case of direct contact we know." And just as if Harman had suspected it, he holds that there is "no second witness to sincerity." [152] This is only logical for an object for which there is no outside.

The pan-object's surplus will be unrealized indefinitely (as is the case in all real objects), making the pan-object irreducible and a guarantor for emergence. Its properties are different and more complex than those of its component-objects. In the same way that a cell can be alive to a degree that its chromosomes or proteins cannot, the pan-object accounts for the surplus of any compound-object: being everything there is, it contains a sincere but indefinite and probably infinite surplus of being. What is going on between the pan-object's components is a mystery to these components as they are unable to exhaust each other, but as a whole the pan-object is condemned to an impossible sincerity.

By showing that agreements are objects allowing for special relations, it was illustrated which problems arise if relations bring forth new objects. OOO is somewhat indifferent on this point: Harman states on multiple occasions that every relation immediately forms a new object, but whether or not a third object is necessary to form a compound object points to a terminological lack of clarity: the term "object" in OOO is sometimes being used synonymously with object-pole (as in "sensual object" or "real object"). In other contexts, it is being used as a moniker for the complete fourfold of sensual object, real object, sensual and real qualities. This leads to a synecdochic conflation of pole and fourfold when discussing objects. It has been explained how vicarious causation between object-poles works, namely through poles of the "opposite" kind: sensual objects act as interfaces between real objects. Real objects never touch directly. But the term "object" evokes a separateness that actually is not the case. Our close analysis of Harman's fourfold diagrammatics shows that a sensual-object-pole must always be part of another fourfold: namely, the real object's fourfold, which it is touching. And even this statement is not entirely precise, since there is no such thing as a "real object's fourfold." At least the sensual poles of every fourfold must be connected to a real counterpart as they would be meaningless without this connection. A sensual-object-pole can only exist as the interface between two objects' real qualities, but this is not reflected in the diagrammatics displayed in *The Quadruple Object*.[153]

If the sensual poles (SO and SQ) can never exist unconnectedly, then what is the case of the real poles (RO and RQ)? This is more complicated. Since the real cannot be accessed directly and is inexhaustible in its relations, the only way to relate to it is by alluding. But how do we know if our allusion is successful? Do we allude to the real or do we just claim to do so? And can all misguided allusion be explained by the mere distortion that inevitably happens in any relations to the real? The real does not answer clearly.

So even though Harman's fourfold looks like a self-contained individual, an individual entity having four poles, its sensual poles can never exist in isolation: and this does not mean in isolation from their three counterparts, but in isolation from at least one other fourfold with which it would share itself. Take the previous example of an international agreement once again, The agreement does have *a* real-object-pole and real accidents, but its sensuality co-depends on the real objects of the underwriting states. If the underwriting states interpret the agreement in very different ways, due to ambiguous wording for example, the reality of the agreement may be in danger. If the parties do not feel bound to the agreement anymore, and no supranational court can enforce its implementation, the agreement effectively ceases to exist; its reality will be no more. But states signing the agreement, not signing the agreement in the first place, or countries opting out later are structurally the same: all these states have a relation to the agreement, either by supporting or rejecting it. For a state not to relate to such an agreement is only possible in a world in which the agreement is non-existent.

To describe these all-encompassing relations, Morton introduces a concept called "the mesh." Both Morton and Harman are in the realm of object-orientation, but Morton focuses more on object relations than objects themselves. Morton's "mesh" is based on two axiom. In his own words: "The First Axiom states, 'Things are made of other things.' The Second Axiom states that 'Things come from other things.'"[154] Morton's stance is relativist and negativist in its definition of objects, but the ontological priority of objects is the same as in Harman's ooo. The "mesh" will unfortunately not help us understand the connectedness of the real poles, as "the mesh is a gridwork of sensual objects rather than real ones."[155] Harman grants the point: "All things are interconnected in the 'weak' sense that they all belong to the same plane of reality, though not in the 'strong' sense of being entirely in contact with everything else."[156] We want to suggest that "sharing the same plane of reality" is a somewhat problematic limitation: if there is one reality, this is obviously the place where all being takes place, but if there were other realities, however defined, this statement suggests there would be no contact at all, not even by means of connecting a real object of this reality to a real object in another, by means of a sensual object able to bridge realities. It is hard not to suspect that through this limitation, the question of definite connectedness of objects is being evaded—erring on the side of objects, and not leaning too much into the supposedly different realm of relations.

From the Impossible Object to the Out-of-Phase Object—Simondon

Using Morton's Second Axiom, "things come from other things," we will move on to explore object generation from existing objects through a description of the "out-of-phase object." We have started our considerations on genesis, identification, and integration in ooo with integration. We found that (1) all objects share common interfaces, since otherwise they would be unable to relate, and (2) all objects are encompassed by an object relating only to itself, an object we named the pan-object. Since relations between objects must be thought of as retroactive effects of the bigger object of which they are part,[157] we can deduce from (1) and (2) that it is the pan-object that provides the interfaces allowing all object to relate. It is the totality of all objects that retroactively allows for relations between all objects.

Harman's diagrammatical object model only accounts for objects' internal workings.[158] While these are discussed thoroughly, the model does not account for object genesis above and beyond making the claim that (nearly) all relations immediately form new objects.[159] However, relation is a term operating on two different orders of magnitude within ooo, namely the relations within and between object fourfolds. While Harman initiated the discussion of the former by calling the fourfold model "a powerful map of the cosmos from which further conclusions can easily be drawn,"[160] the relations between fourfolds have not yet been addressed with such productive rigor.

Both the diagrammatics and terminology of Harman's fourfold conceal the fact that a fourfold cannot exist on its own: his portrayal of objects as independent entities suppresses their necessary integration with neighboring objects. Sensual poles cannot exist simply in relation to their real counterpart-poles within the same fourfold. A sensual-object-pole is always comprised of the influence of (at least) two real-qualities-poles for which it acts as an interface, but only half of these relations is represented in the model. The fourfold cuts off its necessary relations to other fourfolds, thereby representing an effectively impossible object: an unconnected, solitary object, which has sensual object and quality poles but no outside connectivity at all. Harman holds that "Merleau-Ponty [is] a philosopher of perception rather than of objects,"[161] but his famous idealist sentence "I cannot even for an instant imagine an object in itself"[162] is still true, even when applied to the realist quadruple object model.

We assume there are two reasons for this disconnectedness of the model: the first a perceived strategic necessity, and the second is a semantic problem. The strategic reason can be seen in the need to differentiate ooo from process-oriented philosophies and to fend off any gesture that could remotely be regarded as overmining. By having objects take center stage, outside relations as their necessary supporting roles have been disregarded from the model. The only relations displayed in the fourfold are within object-poles—and these relations are not regarded as objects.[163] By trying to prevent the notion of objects as entities being dependent on each other, ooo's object diagrammatics show objects amputated from their neighboring objects, even though they are necessary constitutive parts of those objects. A sensual-object-pole is incomplete without the infusion not of one, but two real-object-poles. If the sensual-object-pole was only connected to the real-object-pole in the same fourfold, it would only relate to itself and such an object would be untouchable, even in the most distorted sense. Devoid of all interfaces, it would signify not just a totally disconnected object, but also a "non-connectable," impossible entity. Harman makes it perfectly clear that "sensual objects would not even exist if they did not exist for me, or for some other agent that expends its energy in taking it seriously."[164] But the "me" that informs the sensual object is not part of the sensual object; it just relates to the sensual-object-pole of the fourfold. However, in order to map the fourfold in its entirety we would need to take the "me" fourfold into account as well. The system forces us to regard both fourfolds together.

In the following, an ooo-compatible thought experiment will be undertaken in which intra-object relations and inter-object tensions are expressed as a fabric of relations. This is a train of thought which, for reasons already mentioned, ooo does not focus on, but which follows conclusively from the model Harman presents. It is alluded to already in *Tool-Being*, where Harman agrees with Heidegger and Whitehead "that an entity is determined by the systematic attachments into which it enters. In other words, there is no absolute line in the sand between monad and global machine. Every entity displays both aspects."[165] We will try to extend the framework for Harman's ontography, his project dealing "with a limited

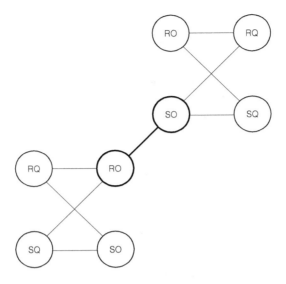

Figure 1

number of dynamics that can occur between all different sorts of objects"[166] by on the one hand stating more precisely that these dynamics take place between object-poles rather than complete fourfolds, and by paving the way to extend these relations across the borders of their "own" fourfold towards their neighboring fourfolds. It is crucial to state that while stressing the importance of relations within and between objects, we do not try to reduce objects to their relations. However, we cannot leave object fourfolds "on their own," since this notion conflicts with the fundamentals of object-oriented ontology itself.

In ooo only objects of the opposite kind can touch. Sensual objects can only touch real objects, and vice versa. But since all objects have sensual and real-object-poles, any object a's sensual-object-pole connects to an object b's real-object-pole (fig. 1).

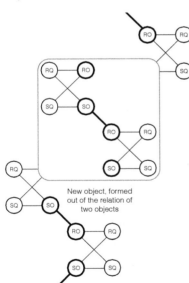

New object, formed out of the relation of two objects

Figure 2

According to ooo, out of any relation between two objects a new object immediately comes forth. This new object again consists of four object-poles and therefore can enter into relations of the same ontological quality than the "lower" objects out of which it was produced (fig. 2).

This move also works the other way around: it is possible to split every object into "smaller" object relations. This however does not mean that splitting it into smaller objects and describing them could ever exhaust an object. Materialist reductionism does not apply, since objects are more than their parts: object-oriented ontology holds that "each domain has its realities, which are not reducible to where they come from."[167] Also, reductionism has to be rejected since the splitting operation can be repeated indefinitely: the tension between two object-poles ontologically takes place

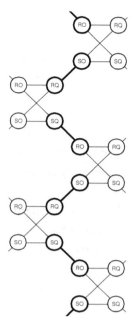

Figure 3

within an object, which contains the two objects touching. These relations are not limited in either direction.[168]

We propose to extend the one-dimensional diagram, which Harman derives from Heidegger's "Geviert," by showing that no fourfold can exist as solitary. We want to achieve this by linking every pole to the proper counterpart in another fourfold. This is the necessary consequence of sensual-object-poles being under the constant influence of (at least) two real-qualities-poles. By adding these relations to the diagram, it becomes clear that fourfolds are always already connected to other fourfolds (see fig. 3).

Fig. 3 is a simplified graph, as any fourfold can interface with an unlimited number of other fourfolds at the same time. When two fourfolds

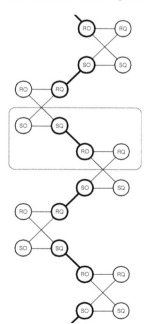

Figure 4

touch, they generate what we will suggest be called an *out-of-phase object*, a hybrid consisting of the sensual-object-pole (so) and the sensual quality pole (sq) of an object a, but the real-object-pole (ro) and the real-qualities-pole (rq) of an object b (see fig. 4).

Is such a hybrid a new object fourfold in its own right? To be a valid object it would need a certain degree of independence from its context and its parts. The sq-ro relation within an object is defined as space. In ooo space and time are not regarded as "peerless dimensions of the cosmos,"[169] but actually as emanating from the tensions within objects: according to ooo, objects are not entities within space and time, but are supposed, for lack of a better term, to establish space and time. An exploration of the out-of-phase-object might be able to shed light on this bold statement.

What is an object, which contains the sensuality of an object a, but the reality of an object b (or the real qualities of object a and the sensual-object-pole of object b)? Let us imagine two sensual objects touching by means of a real object: for example, a spectator experiencing a work of art. "The artwork is not an attempt to approach the real thing outside the mind, this is impossible. You can produce a hybrid identity, where you and the artwork are somehow combined."[170] If this hybrid identity is realized, a new object emerges. But this does not necessarily happen. Obviously, people can encounter works of art without any consequence, so that not every instance of touching generates such a new object (in the strict sense of a durable, independent entity). What inevitably happens in the case of such a non-relation is the emergence of a non-object (as was shown before). The non-object is the residue of the failed emergence of such a new "hybrid identity."

Let us break down how this new object comes forth: the work of art's real object and the spectator's real object touch through their shared sensual-object-pole. The new object that is formed from a spectator's confrontation with a work of art cannot be attributed to only one of the original two objects of which it consists. But instead of just accepting the real object as being a merged entity of both objects involved in the touching, an in-between status is needed. Object-object relations in object-oriented ontology are akin to the model of particles found in physics: a binary system of existence and non-existence. But when viewing objects less like particles and more like waves, as is the case in quantum mechanics, it is much

easier to account for the analog character of object relations—something
we want to propose using the out-of-phase object. Object-object relations
might appear like binary phenomena (either they touch or they do not),
but it seems more reasonable to regard objects as moving like overlapping
sine waves that can be more or less in sync, that can either oscillate
harmonically or not.

Objects being in harmony with themselves is a notion suggested in
Simondon's Genesis of the Individual. Simondon poses a "pre-individual"
state in which a "principle of individuation" already exists, but "in which
there are no steps [phases]."[171] He holds that "internal mediation can occur
as a continuance of the external mediation that is accomplished by the living
individual, thereby allowing the living being to bring two different orders of
magnitude into relation with one another."[172] When applying this model to
objects of all kinds, not just living beings, Simondon explains how a network
of objects works, namely as relations quantized into objects and connected
both on the outside and the inside:

> A piece of information is never relative to a unique and
> homogenous reality, but rather to two orders that are in
> the process of 'disparation.' The piece of information ... is
> never delivered in a format that can be given in a simple
> way. It is the tension between two disparate realities, it is the
> signification that emerges when a process of individuation
> reveals the dimension through which two disparate realities
> realities together become a system. If this is the case, then
> the piece of information acts in fact as an instigation to
> individuation, a necessity to individuate.[173]

Simondon, however, is much more interested in object genesis, since
he holds that the initial incompatibility of an unresolved system "becomes
an organizing dimension in its resolution."[174] The major difference between
Simondon and ooo is that the former posits a pre-individual state: he
explains "the existence of a primitive pre-individual state that is individuated
according to the dictates of the emerging organization."[175] We however
would hold that the pre-individual state is merely a less saturated state
in which the objects involved do not yet have such complex interfaces at
their disposal. In this we contradict Simondon when he holds that "that

the multiplicity of orders of magnitude and the primordial absence of interactive communication between them forms an integral part of any such understanding of being."[176]

While OOO rejects the notion of a pre-individual world, the idea of object genesis by means of the dephasing of a previous entity is perfectly compatible with OOO. As Simondon notes: "Becoming exists as one of the dimensions of the being, that it corresponds to a capacity beings possess of falling out of step with themselves [*se déphaser par rapport à lui-même*], of resolving themselves by the very act of falling out of step."[177]

For Simondon "being" is "a transductive unity, that is, it can pass out of phase with itself, it can—in any area—break its own bounds in relation to its center."[178] The out-of-phase object is the potential quantization of a process into an object, regarded as an object. It is the objects still having to come into existence *for a specific other object* which are of interest here. The above-mentioned spectator ignoring a painting in a museum is not in total oblivion about it. They walk past it, they glimpse it, perhaps only from the corner of their eyes. Georges Didi-Huberman describes this moment:

> To glimpse is to see only in passing: whether something or
> someone moves fleetingly through my field of vision (I am
> at a table in a café, a remarkable being passes in front of me
> and disappears just as quickly into the crowd), or my field of
> vision passes too quickly to linger on something or someone...
> To glimpse, then, is to see the being to be seen just before
> it disappears—a being barely seen, half seen, already lost.
> Already lost, but already loved, or bearing questions, which is
> to say a sort of call.[179]

The glimpse is the moment in which the out-of-phase object can quantize into a stable object, by entering into a relation with the painting. But in extending Watzlawick's famous phrase "one cannot not communicate"[180] to the realm beyond human communication, there is a short moment of contact between spectator and painting. It is in this glimpse that a hybrid identity could form. For a short moment, there flashes the possibility of a relation, of touching. Enter the out-of-phase object: this object state, we want to suggest, attests to the possibility of touching as well as not touching. It represents the probability in the relation or non-relation of objects, an undecided status, which can be thought of as overlapping but still out-of-sync waves before the relation quantizes into a relation—or falls back into a non-relation, forming a non-object, a non-identifiable relation that nevertheless takes part in constituting an object. By introducing this probabilistic aspect into ooo, we on the one hand come closer to the mystery of object genesis from existing objects, and at the same time support ooo with the findings of quantum mechanics, which teach that the probability of a certain event is an amplitudinal function.

Regarding our example, the out-of-phase object is what flickers between both the work of art and the spectator before the relation is either discarded (staying out of phase, establishing a non-object) or established in an identifiable way (entering haecceity). So, Harman's notion of objects being generated immediately from any relation must be re-read with the idea in mind that there is still a relation in failed relations and even in (apparent) non-relations: this relation being *relatability*, Gadamer's *locus of hermeneutics*, quantum mechanics' *amplitudinal probability* or Simondonian *compatibilization*. Compatibility is what ensures the stability of the relata through a shared interface, which is available but not in active use.

The problem with this notion is that such a constant relatability might be misread as a constant undifferentiated relation between all objects, and such a relation would be regarded as overmining, rendering objects useless by sinking them into arbitrariness.[181] However such criticism is based on an equating of relation with relatability. The fact that all objects must be able to touch without touching in the same way or intensity all the time, is important as a fundamental compatibility between objects and also a necessary requirement to cause new objects. But as we will see, even this fundamental compatibility stems from an object performing the activity of compatibilizing. Harman integrates the idea of relations of varying grades of "importance" into ooo in *Immaterialism*.[182] But before looking into this, we want to outline object generation by means of the out-of-phase object.

As long as all objects belong to "the same plane of reality,"[183] they can touch, thus making it impossible to rule out a relation. As Simondon holds, "anything that contributes to establishing relations already belongs to the same mode of existence as the individual."[184] This is also the reason why endosymbiosis as described in *Immaterialism* is possible. The relation of objects as parts of other objects is being examined in Harman's analysis of the serial endosymbiosis theory introduced by Lynn Margulis, who holds that "the organelles inside eukaryotic cells were once independent creatures before later becoming subordinate components of the unified cell."[185] This process effectively creates a whole new organism, depending on the once separate component, a change Harman deems qualitatively different from other interactions during the cell's existence. This new organism is not just the result of the interaction of two different entities, but according to Harman also represents how such an "important" change can make the new organism withstand (potentially dangerous) changes from the outside (in this case the "newly oxygenated atmosphere"),[186] thus making it more independent from its context: this independence being a basic requirement for any object. Simondon describes how two individuals converge by employing the notion of the "collective unit [providing] the resolution of the individual problematic, which means that the basis of the collective reality already forms a part of the individual in the form of the preindividual reality, which remains associated with the individuated reality."[187] So, the fact that endosymbiosis can take place at all is due to the two organisms already being part of a collective system, by sharing common interfaces.[188]

As was shown in the description of the out-of-phase object, this tension of essence (RO-RQ) cannot be the exclusive source of new objects; the SQ-RO and the SO-RQ relations can bring forth new objects as well.[189] This is in line with OOO, as "the primary meaning of 'cause' is to create a new object. Only secondarily does it mean that an object has an effect on others or retroactive impact on its own parts." Harman already alludes to "a 'mereological' view of causation—objects as parts always generating new objects as wholes."[190]

The inexhaustibility of object-relations and the necessary interwovenness of fourfolds into a fabric of fourfolds must include the possibility of any object to touch any other object. There are two ways of generating new objects from overlapping fourfolds: either by way of an SQ-RO or an SO-RQ relation. We will look into both variants, starting with SQ-RO: by regarding the genesis of the out-of-phase object as a process taking place in time, space automatically gets the role of joining two separate objects together. Space is the tension between the real-object-pole of an object A and the sensual-qualities-pole of an object B, which brings forth the new object.

It is however a relation hard to imagine: how, one might ask, could one real object a emanate the sensual qualities of an object b? But instead of looking at the real object emanating sensualities, we need to recognize that a sensual object is the interface of two real objects touching, and that object a already provides its "own" SQ pole. Since the new SQ pole in the out-of-phase object was formerly connected to another fourfold's real object, it had no direct relation to the real-object-pole in question. But the genesis of this out-of-phase object is informed by the sensual qualities' history, since these qualities occur only in the confrontation with another object, which is a quasi-hermeneutic process in time. The object's genesis is thus informed by what Simondon named an object's "milieu," which we would suggest might be extended to cover not just the object's spatial contexts, but its temporal ones as well.[191] Sensual qualities are fleeting, but their history is not lost, and it is precisely this historical milieu—the temporal context—that informs the genesis of a new object.

The second kind of out-of-phase-object is produced by allure and quantizes into an object right away, joining the sensual object (SO) pole of an object a to the real qualities (RQ) pole of an object b. The SO-RQ relation is regarded an object's eidos, signifying the qualities of an object necessary to identify it. As opposed to the painting in the museum, which can be ignored, an SO-RQ relation is more like a sequence in a movie of the Soviet montage tradition: a cut to a new scene immediately reorganizes the content the viewer has just seen, and one is forced to make sense of the new picture, which collides with the previous one.[192] The unity of images progressing through time to form the movie partially falls apart through the unexpected appearance of a new image. The separation is not complete, however: the film has not stopped, both images relate, a movement of the mind ignited in the first scene is continued in the second scene, and both scenes together form a new object that consists in a reframing of the image seen previously, up to the extent of the metanoia-like destruction of an object produced just a second before.[193] Allure is found in the moment of *2001: A Space Odyssey* when the weaponized bone being thrown into the sky by the man-ape is replaced by the spaceship of similar geometry millions of years later.[194] Allure is the perfect collision montage. Successful allure brings two objects oscillating on different wavelengths into a harmonic state, one that is stable enough to endure over time. It is in this moment that Simondon's "compatibilization" of "two orders of magnitude" takes place.[195] It follows conclusively that the method of unpacking the SO-RQ connection is what OOO calls "theory,"[196] a laborious and conscious work of untangling the appearance that, while potentially providing some insight, cannot exhaust the appearance itself, let alone replace it.

Object-oriented ontology allows for uncertainty and inexhaustibility within object fourfolds, but it hardly accounts for these problems when discussing fourfold-fourfold relations. The introduction of the out-of-phase object is an attempt to extend the complexity of the fourfold's internal workings to its outside relations. As mentioned in chapter 1, OOO reverts to a discrete sincerity/nothingness dichotomy in fourfold-fourfold relations. While the complex inner life of objects is necessary to account for the real surplus, the binary structure of the relations between objects is deemed necessary to prevent the world from blurring into an indeterminate lump according to OOO.

To use Gadamer's words, the out-of-phase-object is the "the locus of hermeneutics,"[197] but it is so in a much wider sense, not just as a product of its stability in time and its position far beyond the reader-text relation. The uncertainty of the out-of-phase object's stability reflects the "hermeneutic significance of temporal distance"[198] for object genesis, but Gadamer's time-based notion covers only a fourth of the dimensions in which new objects can come forth: we also have to account for the quasi-hermeneutic processes in the relations of space, essence, and eidos. The discrete differentiation between one object and another is a concept which does not allow for grey values, but the tensions between object-poles as an analog concept do: this is where the space for subtle and virtually unlimited variations is located. This is what the out-of-phase object hints at by extending openness to relations beyond the fourfold's borders. The out-of-phase object is the place where familiarity and strangeness meet on the object level, and given sufficient compatibility in time, space, essence, eidos or a combination of these dimensions, a new object might be generated from the confrontation of the object-poles. The out-of-phase object shows us the potential of a new object emerging and hints at the necessity of any object being capable of touching any other object even at the most distant level, not just in a spatial sense but in all dimensions of relation.

Compatibilization is what makes an object's haecceity while its identity stays inaccessible. Haecceity is found in the activity of compatibilization, but identity stays problematic in a rift that is twofold: it is the rift, namely, between a real-object-pole and its sensual-object-pole (as an interface) as well as the insufficient common interfaces between real-object-poles co-created in the sensual object.

In a certain way, a set of object fourfolds relates to each fourfold of the set in a way that makes the set a new object in its own right. So, objects are at the same time objects in their own right, and part of a set of objects that is another object. But regarding objects as entities containing other objects or being part of a bigger object are spatial metaphors at best, and physicalist reductionist moves at worst. Unfortunately, Simondon is a proponent of such reductionism, which we do not share: "These cohesive forces themselves, which may be taken as the principle of individuation of the complex individual, are in fact negated by the finer structure of the eternal elementary particles, which are the real individuals here."[199] There is no reason why objects should relate to each other in the spatial dimension only. Objects must be able to relate in very different and far more complex ways. The out-of-phase object shows that there is already a flickering and overlapping between objects on the same level. When following the notion of objects being in and out of phase while touching or overlapping with other objects, it becomes clear that objects do not just touch, make a connection or stay disconnected. We need to account for the infinite amount of states between phases. By regarding the relations of objects in the manner of overlapping waves, we get an idea of the impossibility of finding a binary answer to the question of whether two objects touch or not.

Whether objects touch or not then becomes a matter of probability. Thus, in addition to ooo's notion of objects having and not having qualities at the same time, we can now say that all objects touch and do not touch, and not just at the same time as this would forgo the dimensions of space, essence, and eidos. The poles of any fourfolds oscillate in all the relations that up to now exclusively connected the poles within objects. It is not the case that time, space, essence, and eidos are only brought forth by intra-

fourfold relations. It is the oscillation of these four object-poles as interfaces between all objects that bring forth time, space, essence, and eidos. Certain configurations of these dimensions, as long as they can sustain themselves and are somewhat independent from their contents and contexts—as confronted by other objects in the object fabric—are objects. From this vantage point it becomes obvious that the notion of identifiability must be advanced from being dependent on time to being functions of time, space, essence, or eidos. Thus, what an object lacks in stability in time it might make up for by stability in one or more of the other dimensions of relation. Stability is a group effort, a task of an object's milieu.

When regarding touching as a matter of probability we need to adjust the fourfold model to become more like a point cloud of overlapping objects, their poles oscillating in all four dimensions of time, space, essence, and eidos—oscillating between strangeness and familiarity in their relation to other, again oscillating, object-poles. When a certain degree of familiarity is reached, two object-poles interlock and quantize into a new object: in this way the Simondonian "transductive unity" is established.[200] As Simondon puts it:

> The sole principle by which we can be guided is that of the conservation of being through becoming. This conservation is effected by means of the exchanges made between structure and process, proceeding by quantum leaps through a series of successive equilibria.[201]

So, while ooo tends to portray the world of objects as stable from the outside and dynamic on the inside, the ideas introduced in this chapter stress the necessity of extending these dynamics beyond the borders of the fourfold, to the relations between object-poles, regardless of the poles belonging to the same fourfold or not. So while we can hold that the out-of-phase object is an object in its own right as long as it offers interfaces within the object fabric, we have to admit that the out-of-phase object is just the tip of the iceberg of fourfold-fourfold relations. The out-of-phase object c is not necessarily established within time, but can also be a product of the other three relations, and as such it can co-exist to the objects a and b that feed it. a and b can exist in parallel with object c, because time is a sufficient but not necessary dimension of object genesis at all: as we will see in chapter 5, time is much more of an effect of object relations than a mere medium in which these play out.

ooo's offering of "a rare opportunity of reinterpreting space and time in terms of something even more basic: the polarization between objects and their qualities"[202] will eventually lead to an exploration not just of the tensions of time and space, but of an object's essence and eidos.

Chapter 5

Towards the Interface

Giving Signification to the Problem of Disparity

Since we have come to a point where we place an object necessarily within a fabric of objects where all objects are connectable, we need to step back and ask: by focusing on the necessity of this connectivity, have we accidentally discarded objects? How does a fabric of objects differ from an "indeterminate lump" of being? Does it overmine objects by stressing the necessity of their relations?

Simondon differentiates between objects, which he called "individuals," and a "pre-individual" which is not yet individuated, even though a "principle" of individuation is "already active."[203] In the fabric we described there is no non-object, since as we tried to show previously, even non-relations take part in generating relations. So even though a non-object is not thinkable in ooo (including our modest suggestions for extending it) Simondon's notion of "individuation" is useful for understanding how objects come into being in the first place. Does object genesis take place within time? Are all objects always already actualized, as the notion of a fabric seems to imply? Isn't the microbe existent as an object even before Pasteur faces it?

The microbe was already woven into the fabric of objects, but Pasteur was too far away, so to speak, to give signification to it and describe it in a way that would interface within the part of the fabric that is covered by the scientific community. Pasteur's work was that of an interface: this notion, under the term of "compatibilization" between "two orders of magnitude"[204] is a Simondonian concept we want to examine in more detail.

To approach Simondon we utilize the work of Miguel Penas López, who asks what it is that Harman actually rejects when he rejects the notion of the apeiron.[205] To begin, we want to discuss if Simondon's "pre-individual" differs from the *concept* of the *apeiron*. The Pre-Socratic philosopher Anaximander introduced the *apeiron* as the source of all being and the place to which everything eventually returns. Calling it the substance of all things is slightly misleading, since the *apeiron* gives rise to a multitude of substances. However, since all substances can be attributed to the *apeiron*, Harman reads this concept as the rejection of a multitude of substances, and thus as a rejection of the individual (the object). So, while for both Harman and Simondon individuals are the primary reality, the difference in their philosophies becomes obvious when discussing object genesis.

We briefly touched on the problem of object genesis in ooo in chapter 4, which led us to the issue of identification. We also encountered the problem of object genesis in the relativity of any such statement: it was suggested that an object could be regarded as stable (and therefore as an object at all) only as long as its interface does not change. Since the real object is a black box in ooo, we can only determine its stability from the interface it exposes when relating to it in the genesis of a sensual object. The question is if for an object's existence it is necessary not just to *offer* an interface, but actually to *interface* with other objects. Penas López' reading of Simondon supports this notion: "Objects are not the relations they have, but that objects are relations,"[206] Simondon holds. Penas López clarifies: "Every object needs other realities in order to exist and to persist through time."[207] So we know that every relation immediately forms an object in ooo, but how this process works more precisely is unclear. Objects in ooo seem to be justified only in hindsight: once they have proven their independence and stability, they are granted object status. And what made them an object has retroactive effects on what were once separate objects. But if objects became objects only retroactively, would this not grant their relations ontological priority? This would be incompatible with ooo for sure. The solution for this problem, once again, lies in freeing object genesis from being regarded as a process taking place within time.

The descriptions of object genesis in ooo make no statement about how the parts or even their context inform a newly formed compound object. Penas López rightly notes that Harman "does not explain how the genesis of non-intentional real objects is produced, and this is exactly the metaphysical issue that Simondon's philosophy of individuation tries to develop."[208] The question of object genesis, which is the question of individuation, is of particular interest to Simondon. And while Harman focuses on object genesis from existing individuals (i.e. objects), Simondon's goal is "to explain the genesis of the individual and its subsequent individualizations" by "establish[ing] that being is something more than the individual. This is what Harman cannot accept, and the central point of contention is the concept of pre-individual reality."[209]

Here both Penas López and Harman are misled: Harman absolutely accepts, even demands, that objects are always more than just objects. He also accepts that their ability to account for emergence is twofold: they contain a surplus of the real, which is in one pole of any object fourfold, and they are relatively independent of the larger compound object of which they are a part. While Simondon places a surplus of reality on the outside of objects, Harman places it on the inside. So, Harman accounts for the surplus by annexing objects with slivers of ungraspable reality, but without offering any way to classify these slivers as belonging to the unity of a specific real object. He needs to any potential of any fourfold being to be part of it either as its real-object-pole, or as any real-object-pole of any larger compound object the object in question is part of. This repository of future enactability on reality (as we have described the real object in chapter 1), as well as the unpredictability this repository and the relations to other objects bring forth, are what account for emergence in ooo. "Philosophies of the so-called 'pre-individual' treat the world as a semi-articulate lump arbitrarily carved into pieces by the human intellect," Harman holds. [210] This strategy is regarded a variation of reductionist undermining, which cannot account for "the relative independence of objects from their constituent pieces or histories, a phenomenon better known as emergence. An object is not equal to the exact placement of its atoms, since within certain limits these atoms can be replaced, removed, or shifted without changing the object as a whole."[211]

Harman's critique of Simondon is somewhat misplaced, for two reasons. First, the result of this "carving by the human intellect" is no different in what Harman calls the distortion that takes place in the genesis of the sensual object. Second, most confrontations resemble "carving" as they work towards a somewhat "expected" object. This expectation is due to the predefined interfaces that objects expose: objects can confront each other once they share interfaces (a principle that is also at work in the phenomenological method). But when applying ooo's own stance, namely that the process of individuation is in no way limited to the human intellect, the argument against Simondon cannot be upheld. As the squirrel extracts the acorn from the soil or the bat picks up a specific reflection from its ultrasound on a cave's wall, even the way a stone "picks" just the means of confrontation with the water that grinds it down, it is obvious that every object has its own process of confrontation and thus of individuation. This does not contradict ooo, but is perfectly compatible with it. Harman's rejection of the pre-individual must find its basis elsewhere. It seems the pre-individual for Harman has a temporal dimension in two ways: first, he regards the "pre-object" state, which can be overcome by movements of the mind, as pre-existing an object state. There is a sense of a before and an after. Second, the pre-individual also has a simultaneous character: the movement of the mind implies a co-existence of the mind as an individual and the pre-individual from which objects are being carved.

If the arbitrariness of the process of object genesis by the human mind is enough of a reason to refute the pre-individual, we would need to refute all philosophies that allow for intentional objects, as all are prone to arbitrariness. It is perfectly acceptable in ooo to generate arbitrary sensual objects as long as they are co-produced by two real objects, in some cases one of them being the human mind. As long as this particular case of sensual object-production is not regarded as ontologically superior (let alone as the only one there is), ooo should be open to a conceptual infusion from Simondon. Especially when explaining object genesis, Simondon is of great help. Penas López summarizes:

> The individual performs a work of compatibilization, and
> it exists to the extent that it gives signification to what until
> then was only disparity. This work is what characterizes the

> haecceity of every object. It might even be called its identity.
> In any case, this identity is not conceived as some immutable
> traits of an underlying substance, but as an activity of
> mediation. ... Hence, ontogenesis, information, transduction,
> and individuation are different terms for the same process: the
> genesis of the individual and its associated milieu, the activity
> or operation of information, the transduction of a singularity
> in a metastable field.[212]

Metastability is a physical phenomenon used metaphorically: it refers to a system that is not in its lowest state of energy for a prolonged period of time. A metastable system can therefore change at a certain point to another configuration that is energetically more advantageous. Simondon's metastable equilibrium allows for Gadamer's immanent unity of meaning as well as Harman's compound object in ooo: an object comprising objects, which together provide a certain independent stability and provide a unified interface with outside objects. It adds significance to allure.

The ontological question "On What Grounds What?" is the question of ontological priority in which Penas López locates the reason of Harman's discarding of Simondon. Penas López notes that Harman differentiates strongly between the individual and the process of individuation, holding that Simondon prioritizes the latter over the former. However, by discarding the notion of a pre-individual, ooo discards the valuable insights that come with it.

Apparently, Harman reads Simondon as prioritizing relations over objects. He does not acknowledge that Simondon's pre-individual is heterogeneous and therefore not indeterminate. It is not the same everywhere. We suggest reading the Simondonian pre-individual as a surplus of the real, a repository from which distinct sensual objects have not yet come forth. The difference in Simondon's philosophy and ooo is in the extent to which objects are realized on a sensual level at any given time. But when we take seriously Harman's notion of relations actually being "retroactive effects of joint objects uniting [these] two,"[213] we actually get Simondon's principle of individuation:

> [The] principle of individuation has been derived from a
> genesis that works backward, an ontogenesis 'in reverse,'

because in order to account for the genesis of the individual and its defining characteristics one must assume the existence of a first term, a principle, which would provide a sufficient explanation of how the individual had come to be individual and account for its singularity.[214]

This "first term" can be found in the retroactivity of objects—and the pan-object is the realization of this principle. Objects are granted ontological priority because from the pan-object model, it follows conclusively that for every real object there is at least one sensual object being generated in the confrontation with another real object. There are no real objects which do not have at least the possibility of relating to another real object vicariously. The pan-object is a multitude, or to modify a term from Simondon, a field of metastable fields. It is important to recognize the fine line between Simondon's concept of object identity as *what an object does* and our understanding of an object as *which interfaces it provides*. Providing an interface is no activity, it is a potential.

Simondon reimagines the concept of the *apeiron* as "reality of the possible," which Penas López interprets as a "heterogeneity [which] cannot be thought of as 'a semi-liquid, holistic quasi-lump,' "[215] rejecting Harman's critique of processualist philosophies. The heterogeneity of the pre-individual reality makes individuation possible in the first place. Harman's reading could be maintained if Simondon had stopped his research on individuation at this point. But Simondon adds, "Individuation is thus presented as one of the possibilities of the becoming of being, that meets certain defined conditions." These conditions are given in "an interstitial reality which can solve in a unique way the problem posed by the heterogeneity of orders of magnitude," while the object "gives signification" to what was previously "only disparity."[216] But since for Simondon the individual is the "ultimate reality,"[217] and for Harman there is nothing outside of objects, what is the status of that which is not—yet—an object?

We want to suggest interpreting an individual as giving signification not simply to disparity itself, but to the problem of disparity. In this way it becomes clear that Simondon's individual is what Harman refers to as allure: "Allure is the principle of revolution as such, since only allure make quantum leaps from one state of reality into the next by generating a new relation between objects."[218] Making quantum leaps means confronting an object through a new interface. From the perspective of a sensual object the *apeiron* is being dissolved, since the object already mediates between two worlds whose interfaces are well defined by the very object that performs the mediation. Thus, the individual must neither be understood as what carves out arbitrary slivers from the *apeiron*, nor as the principle of solving a problem, but as the principle of naming, of identifying the problem. The necessity of naming (and subsequently solving) a problem is co-dependent on the objects involved. So, when Penas López holds with Simondon that an individual "gives signification" to disparity, we must ask: signification for whom or what? In this way we understand that signification is in the sensual object, and what is not in sensual objects cannot be grasped and therefore cannot be identified. It follows that what is left of the *apeiron* in ooo is what is not (yet) sensually available to a specific object, not even as a problem. The absoluteness of the *apeiron* only stays in the notion that we can never know if there is any other object to which something is significant that appears to us only as disparity. We are like the early zoologists that did not grant any signification to the sounds dolphins make, though this is actually a language and thus very significant to other dolphins.

Distortion as Distortion of Something—Husserl

The notion of an object fabric in the previous chapter was developed by showing how object fourfolds cannot exist in isolation, and by introducing the out-of-phase object as a way to allow object genesis to take place based on existing objects. We also came to the view that non-objects must come forth from all failed relations (i.e. non-relations) as relations to non-objects: relations we called non-relations. These non-relations are as constitutive for an object's identity as are its relations. Non-relations and relations alike form a fabric, which is comprised of the fourfolds described in *The Quadruple Object*. This fabric allows for an explanation of object genesis and integration, and therefore might be able to shed some light on the problem of object identification. Using the fabric we try to illustrate how objects interact, which is necessary to explain a key problem of object-oriented ontology: namely, how it refers to objects which are defined very broadly and vaguely, calling objects somewhat independent from their contexts and inner workings, but declaring this very vagueness a core characteristic of its philosophy. Indeed, Harman regards the problem of the identifiability of objects as a mere "methodological" one because "the difficulty of identifying an object is the whole point [of ooo]."[219] He refers to the inaccessibility of both the real object and its qualities, which prevents direct access to an object's essence, since this is precisely in the tension between these two poles.

This vagueness regarding an object's independence is extended to its mere existence in the sensual realm: "Sensual objects would not even exist if they did not exist for me, or for some other agent that expends its energy in taking it seriously."[220] How do these two notions relate? How do the independence of an object and its dependence on being taken seriously affect each other? The first important point we have to note is that the "seriousness" of a relation is only required from a sensual object. But since we have learned that it is two real objects confronting vicariously through a sensual object that they both co-create, we have to ask: what precisely is it that an agent (which also is a real object) has to take seriously? It cannot be the other real object, since that is not accessible. So, as we saw in the example of the museum visitor becoming aware of a painting but then not paying any further attention to it, a sensual object can form but then disappear. A sensual object therefore must be taken care of (or "taken seriously") in order to persevere. In cases of successful and sustainable generation of a sensual object, both real objects involved in the process must have had compatible interfaces at their disposal, since otherwise there would not have been the slightest chance to create a new sensual object: the relation would have remained a non-relation.

But whatever sensual object is being generated, ooo holds that this sensual object is a distortion of the real object, creating two problems: even when granting that distortion is a production of something new, the notion of the sensual object being merely a distorted version of a real object (1) withholds the fact that there need to be at least two real objects involved in the generation of a sensual object and (2) pretends to have sufficient knowledge to identify the real object which is supposedly being distorted.

Since distortion is always the distortion of an object, we will need to be able to identify distortion as distortion. ooo does not account for different grades of distortion since the real object stays inaccessible, so we suggested identifying objects by tracing them through time; however, we will see that this notion is flawed as well. The problem gets even worse when the question is reversed. How do we know that what we are referring to are two different real objects, when their sensual objects appear the same in confrontation?

If there were multiple identical eidei, it would be impossible to reliably tell objects apart: not just on a phenomenal level, but on the noumenal level (ooo does not explicitly specify whether all eidei must be unique). While it makes sense that any object's essence is unique, since an object's reality can only be enacted once in reality, it cannot be ruled out for different realities to appear the same way in confrontation. Only a sensual object stripped of all influence on the relation to its other (second) real object could reliably identify different real objects as such. Such an unconnected sensual object would however stop existing the moment it loses its relations to the real. As such an object is impossible in the quadruple object model, we are left with the problem that even though there cannot be two identical essences, in ooo one cannot rule out identical eidei.

These issues again demonstrate the seriousness of the problem of identifying real objects. The sensual (the only access to the real) is always under the influence of another real object which makes it not just hard to approach the real object, but impossible to point to any definite object. One cannot even hold that a given sensual object refers to any real object at all, since it is impossible to know (in a case of one-on-one contact) which part of a given phenomenon is substance and which is mere distortion. Ironically, for a philosophy granting objects ontological priority, haecceity in ooo is as fragile as anything.

Of course, one could hold that all object-object relations being taken "seriously" bring forth real objects, and thus can never refer to a non-existent reality. But this would render the substance of the real useless: the sensual and the real would collapse into one, and a host of new problems and paradoxes would appear.[221] Like his teacher Franz Brentano, Husserl holds that consciousness necessarily is consciousness of something, and for him what is given to consciousness is the thing as it is actually given in reality.[222] But by prioritizing the thing in experience ontologically, by placing the real object in experience only, Husserl eventually becomes an "object-oriented idealist."[223] Even though conceived as a realist philosophy, ooo places itself in the Husserlian tradition in some key aspects: giving objects due attention, and applying the phenomenological method to gain access to the *sensual* object: "All ooo can offer on this front are the same sorts of methods that phenomenology offers,"[224] Harman holds. And as for accessing the *real* object, ooo accepts it as a Heideggerian mystery.

By applying the phenomenological method to overcome what the subject puts into the things, one needs to assume the existence of this very object before one can apply eidetic reduction to it. In this way, one creates by correlating what is supposed to be discovered as a true proposition independent of the subject. Husserl made a "simple but far-reaching [point]: the real life of consciousness is occupied with objects, not with sense data."[225] So human consciousness is not occupied with "redness" or "sweetness," but always "gets" unified objects. Harman reads Husserl as saying that "human awareness is riddled with objectifying acts that have already sliced up the world into separate pieces." In *Guerilla Metaphysics*, this is the point on "our ceaseless ventures toward unified objects"[226] where Harman parts ways with phenomenological idealism to hold that it is not consciousness that brings forth unified objects. What is given to consciousness is much rather "already objectively structured in [its] own right, split up into determinate forms from the start."[227]

For Husserl, the process of objectifying takes place in consciousness, and since he holds that these objects are the ones given in reality, his is a thoroughly idealist position. For Harman, real objects exist independently of consciousness (or any form of confrontation). They do however have to be "taken seriously" by other objects in order to generate sensual objects. This leaves open a crucial question: what are the objects "given" to consciousness in ooo? The real objects cannot be given, as they are inaccessible. The sensual object cannot not be regarded as "given" (as in a Cartesian divine guarantee of perceptional correctness) since it is generated in the confrontation of two real objects. But ooo holds that the sensual objects' representation of the real object is always distorted. Distortion however always is distortion of something. We hold that distortion could only be identified as distortion if we knew the baseline object, the real object, the one being distorted. However, in ooo this is not possible.

The phenomenologist works from the inside of an assumed essence, the sensual object, which already is a distorted version of its inherently unknowable real object. One would have to presuppose an essence or in ooo's terms: one would need to have access to the tension between the sensual qualities and the real qualities in order to separate accidents from essence. If one does not know this essence beforehand, the result of any eidetic reduction must be an arbitrary construction, not rooted in any objective reality. Phenomenologists can only discover an essence they deem already there. The phenomenological method provides no hidden path to the real object.

Mathematizing as Practice—Meillassoux and Kolmogorov

It should be noted that the gravity of the problem of identifiability itself is subject to controversy: Harman argues that "if we could identify [an object] with complete certainty then a mathematism such as Meillassoux's would be true."[228] What is meant by this "mathematism"? Meillassoux holds as follows:

> On the one hand, we acknowledge that the sensible only exists as a subject's relation to the world; but on the other hand, we maintain that the mathematizable properties of the object are exempt from the constraint of such a relation, and that they are effectively in the object in the way in which I conceive them, whether I am in relation with this object or not.[229]

Kant held the thing-in-itself, what we would call the real object, to be inaccessible, i.e. unidentifiable, but "imaginable"—a position Meillassoux calls "weak correlationism." Holding the "in-itself" to be unimaginable is what he calls "strong correlationism," a position shared by Wittgenstein and Heidegger. Meillassoux strives to overcome both types of correlationism by positing the mathematical absolute as independent of all correlations. The in-itself can be grasped as long as its properties are mathematizable. Rejecting speculation, the thinking of the absolute, also means rejecting the understanding of the "non-correlationist mode of scientific knowledge." But if one is willing to think the speculative scope of science, one must absolutize the mathematical. For Meillassoux Kant's Copernican revolution actually is a "Ptolemaic counter-revolution," as it overturns the understanding of non-correlationist scientific knowledge.[230] Thus Meillassoux links his philosophy back to Descartes:

> 1. [The Cartesian argument] establishes the existence of an absolute—a perfect God (or what we will call a 'primary absolute'). 2. It derives from this primary absolute the absolute reach of mathematics (or what we will call a 'derivative absolute') by emphasizing that a perfect God would not deceive us. By 'absolute reach' we mean that any aspect of a body that can be thought mathematically (whether through arithmetic or geometry) can exist absolutely outside me. However, if we consider the form which our argument should take, we cannot see any other way of absolutizing mathematical discourse than by accessing an absolute which, even if it is not itself immediately mathematical (e.g. the perfect God), must prove subsequently capable of allowing us to derive the absoluteness of mathematics (e.g. the truthful God who ensures the existence of extended bodies).[231]

Identifying objects with absolute certainty requires accessing an absolute. Meillassoux's philosophy permits this access to the absolute, but only to the conclusion that the absolute is necessarily contingent. According to Meillassoux, mathematics need only adhere to one principle, the principle of non-contradiction, since it is necessary to uphold contingency:

> We claimed that our absolutization of mathematics would conform to the Cartesian model and would proceed by identifying a primary absolute (the analogue of God), from which we would derive a secondary absolute, which is to say, a mathematical absolute (the analogue of extended substance). We have succeeded in identifying a primary absolute (Chaos), but contrary to the veracious God, the former would seem to be incapable of guaranteeing the absoluteness of scientific discourse, since, far from guaranteeing order, it guarantees only the possible destruction of every order.[232]

Descartes, who held that if the methodology outlined in the Discours de la méthode[233] was followed, making absolute statements was possible. At first it seems that both Descartes and Meillassoux allow for certain cognitive processes to bypass the correlation (or distortion). But it is important to differentiate between absolute and complete truths here. This possibility of complete exhaustion would be reserved for an absolute intellect, something we could at best find in the pan-object, a notion that is not part of ooo as it is described today.

In overturning Kant's "Copernican revolution," Meillassoux and Harman share common ground. While Kant would hold that it is unknowable whether mathematics states absolute facts, since this would mean making statements about the thing-in-itself, Meillassoux and Harman do both speculate. It is notable how they differ on what actually limits access to the thing-in-itself. The notion of a mathematical absolute contradicts ooo on a crucial point: Meillassoux allows for undistorted access to certain properties of an object, namely "all those aspects of the object that can give rise to a mathematical thought (to a formula or to digitalization) rather than to a perception or sensation."[234] These aspects, Meillassoux holds, "can be meaningfully turned into properties of the thing not only as it is with me, but also as it is without me."[235] He demands of philosophy that it "[re-absolutizes] the scope of mathematics—thereby remaining, contrary to correlationism, faithful to thought's Copernican de-centering."[236] Mathematizable facts for Meillassoux are not affected by the correlation, but pre-exist any correlation. By applying proper reason, very much in a Cartesian way, Meillassoux allows for the possibility of making absolute statements with regard to certain qualities. These statements are not necessarily true, but "what is mathematically conceivable is absolutely possible."[237] He writes that as long as we do not refer to "color (rather than wavelength), heat (rather than temperature), smell (rather than chemical reactions)"[238] then we are able to make absolute statements:

> Galileo … uncovered, beyond the variations of position and
> speed, the mathematical invariant of movement—that is to
> say, acceleration. From that point on, the world becomes
> exhaustively mathematizable—the mathematizable no longer
> designates an aspect of the world that is essentially immersed

within the non-mathematizable (i.e. a surface or trajectory,
which is merely the surface or trajectory of a moving body),
it now indicates a world capable of autonomy—a world
wherein bodies as well as their movements can be described
independently of their sensible qualities, such as color, smell,
heat, etc.[239]

This sort of absolute is rejected by ooo. In *Immaterialism*, Harman
responds as follows:

> After all, any claim that a thing is convertible into knowledge
> cannot account for the obvious and permanent difference
> between a thing and knowledge of it: if we had perfect
> mathematized knowledge of a dog, this knowledge would still
> not be a dog.[240]

Harman does not contest the claim of being able to make absolute
propositions, but points out that while a complete set of information about
an object, while indeed being an object in its own right, would be a rather
different entity from the object to which it refers.

As was discussed in chapter 1, a completely identical reproduction of
an object would be impossible. A reference to an object (as knowledge
of the object) is a different object as well. Harman holds that "things are
simply not convertible into knowledge, or into any sort of access through
our 'practices,' without significant transformation."[241] Consequently for
Harman mathematics is not a hidden language of the absolute, but a human
practice of describing reality distortedly. But for both philosophers there is
an absolute: for Meillassoux it is mathematics, for Harman it is distortion.

As was shown in chapter 2, informatics (as a variety of mathematics) is
a science of models, which need to be sufficiently practical for a program's
intended use case. Meillassoux perhaps unintentionally alludes to this
problem by demanding a "meaningful" turn of an object into "a formula or
… digitalization."[242] Since meaning is attributed non-absolutely, it can never
be a criterion for a principle of the absolute unless one applies Meillassoux's
own understanding of the absolute: and then the only "meaning" worthy of
the term would be mathematical.

There are two reasons why mathematizability must be rejected as
an absolute property: (1) We insist on the importance of the question

of identifiability because it follows from ooo's object definition of independence that an object must always be something specific and not something else. Would Meillassoux's "mathematism" help identify an object? This would only be the case if an object's identity were a mathematizable quality. But as was described in chapter 1, the object itself is its own primary, unique and sole identifier in the cosmos. So as long as we cannot mathematize the totality of an object, we cannot mathematize the object. (2) Meillassoux's understanding of "mathematization" or "digitization" is problematic. He insinuates that this process is somehow in itself absolute, beyond any correlate. But that is not the case at all: to digitize anything means to design a sufficiently reliable model working at a certain level of abstraction for a specific use case, or in Penas López's words to "give signification to disparity." It is precisely what for Harman would qualify as a distorting practice. Even digitizing in its most mundane form means transferring data from an analog to a digital (discrete) format: for example, when storing musical recordings (as was described in chapter 1). This cannot be achieved without data modeling, which requires arbitrary human decision-making: at which data rate, at which resolution should input be quantized into digital data? Where does one cut off? If one were to digitize for a human audience, one would choose as much auditory data as needed in order for human perception to not recognize a difference from the original performance—a perception of course being limited by specific human sensory capabilities. Digitization is a perfectly arbitrary practice. Meillassoux's usage of the term "mathematizing" betrays the fruitlessness of trying to set up mathematics as an absolute: mathematizing describes a process, a human practice, which is correlationist by definition. A programmer, a person whose work is to bring forth such a meaningful digitization, describes his work as follows:

> Imagine that you are studying a foreign language and you don't know the name of an object. You can describe it with the words that you know, hoping someone will understand what you mean. Isn't this what we do every day with software? We describe the object we have in our mind with a programming language, hoping the description will be clear enough to the compiler or interpreter. If something doesn't work, we bring

up the picture again in our mind and try to understand what
we missed or misdescribed.[243]

The "description," which is a correlationist concept, should be "clear
enough for the compiler or interpreter," which again are correlationist
artifacts, namely computers designed arbitrarily to fulfill certain tasks, which
again are based on human-made concepts of reality. Meillassoux's mere
adequation of property and formula does not exhaust reality; only *equation*
does. This difference is what Harman points out when he contrasts a dog
with its mere description or model.

One could argue here that Meillassoux means digitization not in a
methodological sense, but in a metaphysical one. In this case one would
need to digitize the totality of all mathematizable properties of an object: if
this absolute requirement means the totality of data available to be digitized
(so as to not lose any data) the result would be no digitization at all, but
the thing-in-itself. One cannot digitize without loss. Even so-called lossless
algorithms have to cope with loss, since the moment data is being digitized
(limited by the capabilities of any machinery used to convert from analog
to digital) data is inevitably getting lost. If Meillassoux held that his notion
of digitizing was meant to signify finding proper algorithms to map reality
onto an algorithm, the problem would persist, for three reasons: (1) The
impossibility of mathematizing without modeling (as shown in chapter 2),
(2) the necessity for the input of discrete data, which is antithetical to the
infinite regression of the objects in the world as it is given (a model cannot
work with the totality of anything, but only with a quantized and thus
arbitrarily reduced subset of reality turned into discrete data), and (3) the
Kolmogorov complexity of such an algorithm, which we will now examine in
more detail.

The mathematization of complex objects, let alone of what we called
the pan-object, is not just impossible because a mathematical description
never equals described reality, but because the very requirements of such a
description rule out the possibility of meaningful mathematization in itself.
To support this statement, we want to make use of algorithmic information
theory's concept of Kolmogorov complexity. An object's Kolmogorov
complexity (K) is the length of the shortest computer program (or
algorithm) that is able to generate this precise object ("object" in the sense

of information theory, not in the ooo sense). The more complex an object, the larger its Kolmogorov complexity. One could call K the amount of work necessary to mathematize an object.

As an example, the string s1 which consists of abcabcabacbabcabcabcabcabcabc and is 30 characters long, can be turned losslessly into the (pseudocode) algorithm k(s1) repeat ab 10 times. k(s1) is only 18 characters long. And while s1 and k(s1) are different objects, the output of k(s1) is identical (again, in information theory terms) to s1. When attempting to turn a more complex string into an algorithm—let us call it s2 and have it contain oqorgvg6wpcm30vᴇ—one would most likely end up with an algorithm k(s2) merely repeating the original string, like print oqorgvg6wpcm30ve, as there is no shorter way of producing the data given.

In other words, the only algorithm representing a given reality in its entirety is no algorithm but reality itself. To use ooo's terms, no algorithm—being a sensual object and acting as an interface—can ever exhaust any real object. No algorithm can handle the surplus of the real. The real is not mathematizable.

Sincere Distortion, Meta-Confrontation

While for Meillassoux mathematizable properties are absolutes, Harman holds the same of the distortion that takes place in confrontation. To understand this distortion, we want to look at ooo's opposite concept, sincerity. In his 2005 book *Guerilla Metaphysics*, five years before introducing the quadruple object in the book of the same name, Harman describes sincerity as having two functions, on the one hand "an adhesive: a powerful glue cementing subject and object to such an extent that they no longer appear separable"[244] and on the other hand "its selective side": conscious experience "also binds [subject and object] in a very specific way, and even defines itself by what it experiences."[245] This obviously is not yet the same technical definition of the impossible sincerity, which can be found in the fourfolds as described in *The Quadruple Object*, but it is still helpful since it highlights two crucial aspects of identifying objects.

The subject and object bound together (or object and object, since Harman later seems to drop the subject term for good) is what was to become the sensual object, the object existing only in experience (or in "confrontation" as the relation will be called in *The Quadruple Object*). The perspective on how to regard this binding has changed over the years. In a 2010 article Harman holds that object relations are actually "retroactive effects of a joint object that unites the two."[246] This change of perspective allowed us to posit that all object-poles must share a common interface, because within ooo it must be possible to posit an all-encompassing pan-object accounting for the relations retroactively established between all object fourfolds.

When we say that object-poles must share a common interface, we encounter a specific problem of the inaccessibility of the real. Since ooo holds that the real exists as distinctive, independent objects to which other real objects only gain access in a distorted way, it implicitly makes statements about these real, inaccessible objects. ooo posits an absolute knowledge not of the specific nature of distortion, but of the *existence* of the distortion that takes place in relations between object-poles. Distortion always refers to a *specific* object in the same way intension is always directed towards a specific object. ooo holds that a sensual-object-pole is always informed by the real-object-poles it vicariously connects. These relations fail to grasp the real in its entirety, but the reference seemingly never fails to relate to specific real objects. The sensual may be a grotesquely skewed version of the real, but as long as the relation exists, it brings forth a version that is somehow informed by the real objects involved. What follows is a downright incredible certainty in the two distortions' directionalities: unless one holds that the distorted object is completely detached from the real object (a position negating ooo's concept of relative stability), the distortions must be informed by the real object's limitations regarding the other real object confronted, e.g. the subject's presuppositions or expectations. How can we uphold that the real object coming forth from such constructions (this term used with all necessary caution) pre-exists the confrontation? Would we not become idealists holding that not just the sensual object, but the real object is only generated in confrontation?

While ooo is probably the only form of speculative realism worthy of the "realism" label (since it advocates for a reality independent of human access), it also maintains Kant's thing-in-itself under the terminology of the real object. But even though ooo deems the real object inaccessible, it does imply direct access to the distortion between the real and the sensual object. So, while we can only "allude" to the real object, our relation to the distortion is sincere. The question is: can one ever relate to a distortion as if it were an object in its own right and not just the quality of a relation?

To approach this question, we need to consider the nature of distortion. OOO has to posit distortion as absolute, since it needs to guarantee objects the ability to confront other specific real objects. But what is distortion if not the difference between the sincere relation to be found on the inside of an object fourfold (the immediate, object-internal SO-RO relation) and the relation as coming forth from real and sensual-object-poles whose poles reside in different fourfolds? Since the sincere relation can only take place within a fourfold, all relations involving more than one fourfold are necessarily distorted. And since Harman deems the direct, "sincere" relation impossible,[247] it is also impossible to generate knowledge on the baseline to compare it to the distorted relation. But by assuming the existence of the distortion, do we not necessarily have some knowledge about the nature of the distortion, and thus indirectly about the undistorted real object as well? We most certainly do, and this is because we have access to other objects confronting the object in question, acting as stabilizing agents for our otherwise fragile relation. The distortions, being an absolute knowledge that OOO posits, allow us to approach the real objects behind the distortions. By combining knowledge about the distortions, we can, if not cancel them out, at least hedge the real objects behind them.

We want to suggest the following. If there is a sincere relation within an object fourfold (the SO-RO relation) and a distorted one between the real-object-pole of fourfold a and the sensual-object-pole of a fourfold b, and the fourfold a were to enter into relations not just with a fourfold b, but also with fourfolds c, d, e, and so on, and we (being is represented in a fourfold z) can relate to these confrontations, by inquiring into the confrontations (a-b)-z, (a-c)-z, (a-d)-z, (a-e)-z and so on, we would be able to approach the distortions that define these confrontations. By *confronting the confrontations* with the object in question, we improve the chances of distortions cancelling each other out or at least overlap in a way that makes it possible to approach the real object in a gradually more adequate way. Meta-confrontation should not be regarded as a methodological approach to the problem of identification (a mere variety of Husserl's eidetic reduction), but a fundamental ontological concept that follows necessarily from the idea of an object fabric.

Since knowledge is limited by the capabilities of sensual objects, it can never be objective. Intersubjective facts can be generated in cases where primary qualities (as weight) are involved, but when this epistemic process is regarded as playing out on only one level, in one province of the fabric, it becomes clear that the knowledge coming forth, even though relatively stable (and therefore an object in its own right) can never claim absoluteness. The possibility of meta-confrontation strengthens an ontology of shared interfaces. The extent of an object's independence from its inner workings and outer contexts becomes much easier to grasp when regarded as the extent to which an object confronts other objects. A weak connection to one object can be compensated for by a stronger connection to another one. The amount and complexity of interfaces an object provides, and how much is being made use of them, are therefore indicative of its stability.

This stability revealed in meta-confrontation is at the root of an object's ability to identify objects as specific objects, similar to checksum functions in informatics. A checksum is a piece of data used to detect errors in storage or transmission or to compare larger datasets without comparing every single byte of them. It works like an object's fingerprint, which does not contain the object in its entirety, but enough information so as to not confuse it with another object. It is not possible to deduce the complete object just from knowing the checksum, but it is possible to *identify* an object with almost complete certainty. The checksum function, which is communication on communication, works similar to an object's eidos. It is produced in the confrontation of the sensual objects with its real qualities; it allows for identification without giving away its entirety. But when thought of as a result of meta-confrontation, by taking the multitude of confrontations into account, the eidos becomes more stable and more saturated, leading to a richer relation between sensual and real qualities, a more reliable checksum.

There is a peculiar relation between genesis and identification. If we think of real objects as having unique signatures (themselves), which are always distorted in the sensual object they co-establish, we become aware of the unidirectional nature of identification. The two real object's' signatures are both inputs of the process forming the sensual object. This process of confrontation happens "on its own," while its reversal is very difficult. But when regarding the "adhesive" of sincerity as a merely retroactive effect on the inside of a compound-object, it becomes clear that a sensual object's genesis is to its identification what multiplication is to prime decomposition: the way there is easy, the reverse journey is incredibly hard. It follows from the vicarious structure of the fabric of objects that the genesis of its parts is the very reason they become inaccessible when trying to access them separately. Thus, when we ask what we mean when we inquire about *this object*, it is a structure that answers.

Hedging Essence—Object-Poles Stabilizing Each Other

In chapter 4 it was found that in order to grant objects independence, it is necessary to integrate them into a fabric of neighboring objects. It follows that object fourfolds cannot exist as solitary and that the relations within fourfolds, which represent time, space, essence, and eidos, must be thought of as extended to other fourfolds. We therefore want to make use of this "rare opportunity of reinterpreting space and time [as] the polarization between objects and their qualities."[248] In doing so, we want to take into account that relations between object-poles are not the result of confrontation, but are a retroactive effect of a pre-existing compound-object of which these poles are already parts. We will therefore need to reconsider Gadamer's hermeneutics, which holds that time needs to pass in order for an object to become an object in the first place.

The world we describe here is a fabric of fourfolds, a flexible but rigid structure in which real, rigid cores and their sensualities confronting each other are interlinked, but without granting ontological priority to either the real or the sensual. This position is supported by Penas López's notion that "every object needs other realities in order to exist."[249] Penas López, summarizing Simondon, holds as follows: "An individual is a place of communication; therefore, a relation is a movement from the outside to the inside which constitutes and sustains the individual, an operation which produces a structure."[250] If a relation is an operation producing a structure, this structure is a structure between objects. Penas López only alludes to the fact that objects need to provide interfaces in order to communicate. What we will try to show is that this communicating fabric follows necessarily from the assumptions that ooo makes, and that it eventually leads to a self-stabilizing structure. This structure we want to introduce is an object-fabric where the fabric informs and stabilizes the objects without depriving them of their ontological priority.

A real object depends on a sensual object's capability of confronting other objects, but it is not just the interface the real object provides that defines the nature of such a confrontation. Rather, it is the fabric of object relations, which defines how objects can touch. The objects themselves form the fabric, which again forms the conditions of object confrontation: Lambert Wiesing suggests that it is not the subject constructing its perception (the idealist stance), but perception constructing the subject.[251] We want to hold that the interfaces we dispose of, namely the sensual objects, co-create sensual and therefore real objects. It is the interfaces between objects that allow for a fabric of all objects, which stabilizes reality. The reason why there is some stability at all in the cosmos (or a series of Simondonian "metastable equilibria") is due to a structure with which all objects on the same plane of reality must have interfaces. These stable, reliably relatable, identifiable objects (through meta-confrontation) we want to call "facts," knowing that this is a term which lately has come under political fire. Also, in order to play a modest part in rehabilitating this term, we want to suggest a portmanteau composed of the terms "interface" and "fact" and name this all-encompassing, stabilizing structure the "interfact."

In order to justify the necessity of the interfact we must acknowledge the problems introduced in this chapter: (1) ooo's lack of acknowledgment of the multitude of both real and sensual objects being involved in the generation of a sensual object and (2) the idea of distortion being a distortion of something, but of something that cannot be attained, not even by applying the phenomenological method since it puts the correlation with the subject into the real object, thus making it impossible to recognize distortion as distortion.

What we suggest is to use the idea of meta-confrontation so as to regard object relations as converging sensual objects "hedging" real objects. This is especially necessary in order to identify an object's essence, which is in the completely withdrawn tension between a real-object-pole and its real-qualities-pole (RO-RQ). The notion of hedging acknowledges OOO's realism in its acceptance of real objects independent of experience. But we want to underline that the genesis of sensual objects is a group effort, contingent on the participation of a multitude of object fourfolds on any sort of level— spatial, temporal, eidetic, and essential on the horizontal level as well as on the vertical level (on which the object relates to the compound-object it is part of). And instead of the obvious invoking of human intersubjectivity alone, we want to stay true to the non-anthropocentric speculation of OOO and require every object to participate in the hedging of real objects.

The interfact is a self-stabilizing structure of objects comprised of the (speculative) epistemic processes taking place between objects. The interfact is not correlationist because it does not depend on a human-world relation. The interfact does not deny objects ontological priority, but acknowledges that objects, as described in Harman's Fourfold, are always "half-sensual." The interfact is the reason an object can be identified at all, but in no way does it guarantee this possibility. The interfact is also not equally dense everywhere, meaning that there can be a lot of epistemic processes taking place in one zone but close to none somewhere else (or even none at all, when taking into account the possibility of "dormant objects"). The interfact is why some objects can be identified more easily than others, and why a certain density and configuration of objects constitutes what we call "facts."

While it is true that a sensual object comes forth in the relation between two real objects, the problem of identifying the real object can only be sufficiently explained by incorporating all relations into which any real object can enter, including second-degree touching (and third and so forth). For the concept of the interfact it is insignificant who or what the objects in it are. But it is easier to pick examples from the realm of a human subject's relation to other objects as from non-human interactions, so this is what we will now do.

If we want to make sure we are referring to something meaningful by talking about the water in the glass on the table, we do not just relate to the water in the glass, but to the other relations into which the water enters with its surroundings. We relate to the glass, keeping the water in its upright form. We relate to the sun slowly evaporating the water. We relate to the friend that handed us the glass, to the chemical knowledge we have about the water's composition; we use language to communicate about the glass. However, we do not reduce the water in the glass to its mere effects on its surroundings, since our invoking of the water's relations is primarily used to hedge its real object. Again, we do not hold the water to be exhaustible by its relations. However, by taking second order relations into account, we leverage the stability already realized within other fourfold-fourfold relations, a stability necessary for objects to become complete and not just real objects at all. This leveraging allows us to refer to a real object even though we do not have direct access. We suggest acknowledging the multitude of interwoven vicarious relations available. This way we saturate the sensual objects we co-create. Object stability (or independence) is a function of the interfaces involved, interfaces that quantize unstable relations (out-of-phase objects) into "metastable equilibria." The more relations into which an object can enter, the more saturated it becomes, the more substantial a statement about the object becomes, the more likely that it turns into what one could call a fact.

To place this notion in the phenomenological tradition, one could posit that instead of stripping away accidents from objects we allegedly do not know, we suggest incorporating the whole surrounding of an object so that it doesn't slip away. Simondon invokes the notion of the "milieu" that surrounds every individual: "There exists within the being a more complete regime of internal resonance requiring permanent communication and maintaining a metastability that is the precondition of life."[252] The communication Simondon describes is made possible by the interfaces that objects provide, and while ooo would extend this description to non-living objects as well, it provides an accurate description of the infinite regress in every object consisting of component objects (the vertical integration) which are objects in their own right, maintaining stability and establishing permanent communication.

The milieu is what makes identification, if not possible, then at least more likely: "The milieu is itself a system, a synthetic grouping of two or more levels of reality that did not communicate with each other before individuation."[253] If one leaves out the notion of individuation implying a pre-individual state, which ooo rejects, we can hold that the milieu is a compound object, but not just in a spatial sense, but a compound also acting out in time as well as the relations of essence and eidos.

Simondon uses a plant as an example of this communication between two "orders of magnitude": "A plant institutes a mediation between a cosmic order and an inframolecular order. Classifying and distributing the different chemicals contained in the soil and the atmosphere by means of the solar energy obtained from photo-synthesis."[254] One of the main functions of the individual for Simondon is "becoming," which is "one of the dimensions of the being, a mode of resolving an initial incompatibility that was rife with potentials."[255] From Simondon we want to adopt the idea of objects as resolvers of incompatibilities between other objects. This is the function that objects fulfill in the interfact—"resolving incompatibilities" is a technical term for ooo's vicarious causation. This interfacing is also precisely what objects do in object-oriented programming.

Object independence is maintained by the interfact, since object fourfolds still represent inexhaustible entities: using terminology from network theory, we can easily see that object-poles are nodes, while the tensions are edges in a network. This very terminology is employed already by Simondon: "The living being can be considered to be a node of information that is being transmitted inside itself—it is a system within a system, containing within itself a mediation between two different orders of magnitude."[256]

Harman holds that "partial autonomy has yet to be explained."[257] We want to offer the following explanation. Stability and independence are interdependent forces: independent nodes are only "somewhat" independent. They can move as long as they stay connected to other nodes. But since we stated that no object-pole can be entirely disconnected, we must hold that a node a that loses its connection to node b necessarily must connect to another node c, leading to the insight that if something ceases to be an object for me, it becomes an object for someone or something else. Nothing can fail to be an object (as even non-objects are objects in their being an object-codefining failed relation), and being an object always means being an object for another object. This again explains why the same object can behave in opposite ways in different situations. It depends on its context, or in networking terms: its neighboring nodes. It should be obvious by now that an ontology based on objects as defined in OOO necessarily leads to a network of objects, a network we have come to call the interface.

"It seems as if object-oriented philosophy must be complemented with a process-oriented philosophy, just as process philosophy must make space for enduring objects," Penas López holds.[258] We do not make this point here, since we hold that if object-oriented philosophy acknowledged the connectivity of object-fourfolds—which follows logically from OOO itself—it could address the problem of object identification and genesis elegantly and without removing ontological priority from objects. If we regard objects as interwoven in a multidimensional structure, we can show how object-poles stabilize each other, making for an epistemically identifiable reality. Objects that share common interfaces allow for rich explanations of interactions (including complex and non-gradual changes like endosymbiosis) without resorting to a process-centric philosophy. As Harman warns, "if we treat every relation as significant for its relata, we slip into a 'gradualist' ontology in which every moment is just as important as every other."[259] This problem can also be countered by using the notion of interfaces: while objects can change (in insignificant ways), the moment their interfaces change, they become significantly different. The same mechanism is at work in object genesis as described by Simondon: by compatibilizing between different orders of magnitude, objects become significant. The reason they can enact this reality is that the objects involved share fundamental interfaces. Object genesis is contingent on common interfaces. Neither are all objects "the same," nor are all of them always connected (or "One"), but all are fundamentally connectable.

When we say that objects are somewhat independent from their inner workings and outer contexts, we imply that we know the borders of the object. But these borders between the object and its neighbors need to be "renegotiated" constantly. It is in these "negotiations" that objects become objects, since their relative independence only means independence from their neighbors.

Retroactivity—Beyond Under- and Overmining

If time is the SO-SQ tension and takes place entirely in sensuality, it cannot be one of the mathematizable (primary) qualities of objects (at least not if one subscribes to Meillassoux's position). It would be contradictory to allow for time and space to be objective realities as omnipresent media, which is why Harman suggests that we overcome the notion that they are "peerless dimensions of the cosmos."[260]

Referring to Simondon's plant example of compatibilizations, Penas López notes "two questions haunting [his] reading of Harman's object-oriented ontology: how is the genesis of the plant explained? Once the plant is already individuated, how can we explain its successive transformations without appealing to a reality outside the plant?"[261] An answer might be found in reading compatibilization not (just) as a process in time, but as a given state shared by all objects by virtue of the retroactive existence of the pan-object. The notion of the interface again might help shift our attention towards the outside relations of objects being part of compound objects. But we need to expand the notion of compounds to account for relations beyond the spatial dimension.

Since all relations are retroactive effects of compound objects, of which every object always already is a part (as what we call component-objects), all objects eventually are component-objects of a pan-object encompassing all objects. Thus, all inter-object relations are actually intra-object relations of compound objects, maintaining ontological priority of objects over relations. We will use the term "actually" with caution, since we do not want to fall prey to the tendency of reducing one object or relation to another, seemingly ontologically superior one. Since relations (which were shown to be extended to inter-fourfold relations) become retroactive effects of compound objects as well, we are led to the most peculiar result: not just time and space, but also an object's essence and eidos must be thought of as consequences of object-poles confronting each other:

> [Space and time] are the tension of identity-in-difference, the strife between real objects and their accidents (space) or intentional objects and their accidents (time). And since under this model both space and time involve accidents as one of their poles, in a sense it is true that both are forms of perception, and Kant was right to say so—though only in a Kantianism extended beyond humans to flowers and inanimate things. Under this model, time and space are not

primordial givens of the cosmos but are derived from the inherent metaphysical tension between objects and their qualities.[262]

When rethinking time as an effect, not a medium of object interaction (as was suggested in chapter 3), the method of identification changes dramatically. We lose the medium of identification, because it would only come into existence by the very relations that constitute the compound object we are trying to trace in the first place. Taking time and space seriously as "[arising] from the tensions between things and their qualities,"[263] being consequences rather than absolute media, we can state the following: both are regarded as mere effects of object-poles relating, the RO-SQ tension establishing space, the SO-SQ tension establishing time.[264] But since fourfolds are integrated into a fabric of fourfolds, the space and time tensions need to be regarded as extended beyond a fourfold's borders, connecting not just object-poles, but complete fourfolds to other fourfolds.

It is important though to note that in this context the term of retroactivity does not refer to a process in time but is to be understood as an ontological generality: object genesis is informed by a Simondonian "milieu," which is what OOO calls a compound object. In OOO, the milieu is a retroactive effect of any object relation and it is precisely this retroactive effect, which allows for object identification. And just as the cell is a milieu for the organelles it contains, objects also are milieus for other objects. Objects in Simondon's sense "compatibilise" between different "orders of magnitude." Since all objects are retroactive effects of compound objects ("milieu"), and all milieus in turn are retroactive effects of larger milieux (larger not just in a spatial sense, but in all relations objects can enter into), the interface becomes a multidimensional structure resolving Heideggerian *Vorhandenheit* into local *Zuhandenheit*.

The interface, even though it covers all objects, does not exhaust them: it is a fabric of interconnected fourfolds, whose poles form a probabilistic point cloud, thus generating time and space as local phenomena, and any fourfold's eidos and even essence under the influence of the surrounding fourfolds in the fabric. The element of probability accounts for (1) the fact that not every object is connected to every other object in the same way or same degree of "importance," (2) the impossibility of making absolute and complete statements about the real-object-pole, thus not being exhaustive, and (3) the necessity of connectability of all objects on the same plane of reality, which we have called interfaceability.

The notion of retroactivity seemingly evokes a contradiction of a basic principle of ooo: namely, the ontological priority of the object. One could ask: how is reducing relations between objects to retroactive effects of larger compound objects not a form of overmining? The relations between objects are dismissed as mere retroactive effects, meaning that some larger object is at the root of the smaller object's behavior. How can we uphold the notion that ooo doesn't employ a hierarchical structure when we are supposed to "explain away" relations by reducing them to retroactive effects of a larger compound object? One might reply that component objects are not being reduced to compound objects; anyhow, they retain all their ontological capabilities including their relative independence. But this integration of objects not only poses the question of supervenience (do the parts command the compound ontologically or vice versa or is it a mere relationship of reciprocal mapping?). Imagining compound objects as objects containing others in a spatial sense is an arbitrary, though intuitively understandable metaphor. ooo, however, has a preference for the spatial dimension, not just when describing compound objects (which "contain" each other), but also when rejecting alternative philosophies altogether. Undermining, the strategy of rejecting naive materialism, takes place in the spatial dimension. So does overmining, but in a metaphorical as well as a literal sense: rejecting structuralism works by criticizing a focus on larger contexts, which can either be acted out in space or in more complex structures like societies. But even then, the notion of covering more or less ground or volume is omnipresent. Both undermining and overmining are negative strategies, which serve their duty in rejecting philosophical alternatives ooo dismisses. Their rejection can not lead the way to the further development of ooo. By focusing on rejecting alternatives in the spatial dimension, we are prone to overlook the other three dimensions that come forth in object relations: in order to expand the fourfold model once again we want to make the case that it is not just space and time, but also essence and eidos which have to be understood as consequences of object interaction.

The rationale behind this proposal is as follows: if we (1) want to preserve objects' ontological priority, (2) reject an ontological hierarchy of objects, (3) accept that object-pole relations are just retroactive effects of compound objects and (4) speculatively allow for confrontations far beyond human-world confrontation, we need to face the music. The fourfold theory falls short of itself when it fails to acknowledge the other dimensions besides space when explaining compound objects, and time when explaining object genesis.

Conclusion

Object-oriented ontology is a realist philosophy that grants objects ontological priority and defines them as distinct entities that are to a certain extent independent from both their inner workings as well as their context. Hence, it should be a simple task for OOO to refer to objects. But this is far from being the case, as "the difficulty of identifying an object is the whole point."[265]

After introducing the basic concepts of OOO in chapter 1, we began addressing the problem of an object's haecceity, its "thisness," with an investigation into OOO's eponymous practice, object-oriented programming (OOP): we found not just a plethora of parallels, which we outlined in chapter 2, but eventually identified OOP's concept of interfaces as a most promising tool to describe the rift between objects, which is a key characteristic of OOO. Interfaces are structured ways of object confrontation guaranteeing communication over a period of time.

This concept lead us to the exploration of the relation between time and the possibility of identifying an object as an object, which was conducted in chapter 3. We referred to Gadamer's hermeneutics to discuss the relation between the passing of time and the making of meaning. The concept of meaning as a relation of intension and extension was discussed using the works of Putnam and Kripke, leading us to the co-creation of sensual objects.

In chapter 4 we developed the notion of objects being necessarily *relatable*. Integrating Bhaskar's rejection of ontological monovalence, we distinguished objects from non-objects, the latter—even though unidentifiable—being essential for object genesis and identification. Based on these thoughts we developed the necessity of object integration into a fabric of sorts. This fabric must be thought of as existing in both a horizontal dimension (of interconnected, overlapping object-fourfolds) and a vertical dimension (objects always being part of larger compound objects). Applying Harman's stance that objects are merely retroactive effects of compound objects, we developed the necessity of a compound object encompassing all objects, which we named the pan-object. The pan-object realizes the ultimate sincerity, the one with itself, and thus guarantees the stability of the overall structure. We then criticized the fourfold diagrammatics as laid out in *The Quadruple Object* by noting the self-contradictory nature of its object model, which depends on the relations between objects, but nevertheless treats object-fourfolds as solitary entities (especially in the diagrams employed in the book). These diagrams depict objects that are impossible by ooo's own standards. We also criticized usage of the term "object" for both object-fourfolds and object-poles in *The Quadruple Object*, causing confusion and concealing the interconnectedness of object-fourfolds to other object-fourfolds. We therefore suggested the extension of the fourfold diagram to reflect the necessary linkages between fourfolds. This led to the introduction of a new concept of object genesis, the out-of-phase object, based on the observation that fourfolds, when displayed in a manner true to ooo's description, are always already parts of other fourfolds. The out-of-phase object then appears as a probabilistic object, a potential that *can* quantize into a stable object but need not do so. This concept was likened to phenomena as different as quantum mechanics, Didi-Huberman's "glimpses," and eventually Simondon's notion of individuals "resolving themselves by the very act of falling out of step."[266]

Consequently, in chapter 5 we undertook a critical reading of Penas López' comparison of Harman's and Simondon's concepts of the individual. Simondon's notions of the milieu and the pre-individual stress an object's interwovenness in time and space, which for ooo are mere consequences of object relations. It is Simondon's concept of compatibilization, giving objects their identity, which we want to make usable for ooo. Objects give signification to *the problem of* disparity: by compatibilizing between other objects they end disparity and perform the revolutionary act of *allure* as described by ooo.

After rejecting Meillassoux's absolutization of mathematizable properties by reducing digitization to a human practice, we showed that ooo too is prone to absolutizations, which can be found in its concept of distortion in object confrontation. However, knowledge about an ever-present distortion can be used to hedge inaccessible essences by confronting confrontations (meta-confrontation), eventually leading us to the concept of the interface.

This multidimensional structure solves the problem of object identification by recognizing the confrontation between object fourfolds as overlaps, which can again be confronted. By regarding all objects as interwoven into such a fabric, it becomes obvious that objects support each other: a stronger node compensates for a weaker one somewhere else in one of the dimensions of space, time, the relations forming an object's essence and eidos, as well as the object-compound-object relation. By taking meta-confrontation into account, essences can be "hedged," thus becoming more identifiable, resolving more non-objects into objects and making for more saturated sensual objects, the basis for what we call facts.

The work ends with a speculation on the consequences of the interface, which gives rise to a thought that overcomes the spatial and temporal metaphors in object-oriented ontology (undermining, overmining, compound objects, retroactivity). We suggest further research to explore the idea of compound objects not just containing component objects on a spatial level, but also on temporal, essential, and eidetic levels as well. This also demands a more suitable vocabulary than "compounds" and "containing," which would still have to be developed. Similar to using "confrontation" to cover the relations and rifts between all objects, we need a new term to free object-oriented ontology from the metaphorical shackles that tie it to the spatial and temporal dimensions.

ooo is an ontology inconceivable without the speculative epistemic processes between objects. As long as we remain unimpressed by hasty and unjustified accusations of correlationism, the investigation of the ontological consequences of epistemic processes between objects could be a fruitful project. The interfact, we hope, is a modest first proposal with which to start this endeavor.

Notes

1. Immanuel Kant, *Critique of Pure Reason*, ed. Paul Guyer and Allen W. Wood, The Cambridge Edition of the Works of Immanuel Kant (Cambridge: Cambridge University Press, 1998), A805/B833.

2. Ray Brassier, Iain Hamilton Grant, Graham Harman, and Quentin Meillassoux, "Speculative Realism," in *Collapse*, ed. Robin Mackay, vol. III (Oxford: Urbanomic, 2007), 308.

3. Kant, *CPR*, Kant, *CPR*, B xiv.

4. Graham Harman, Personal communication, March 12, 2017.

5. Graham Harman, *The Quadruple Object* (Winchester, U.K.: Zero Books, 2011).

6. Harman, *The Quadruple Object*, 124.

7. Harman, 130.

8. Classical semiotics denies certain phenomena (like biological reflexes) the status of a sign, while ooo does not have this limitation.

9. Umberto Eco, *Opera aperta: forma e indeterminazione nelle poetiche contemporanee* (Milan: Bompiani, 2013).

10. Ian Bogost, *Alien Phenomenology, or, What It's like to Be a Thing*, Posthumanities 20 (Minneapolis: University of Minnesota Press, 2012), 23.

11. David M. Berry, *Critical Theory and the Digital*, Critical Theory and Contemporary Society (New York: Bloomsbury, 2014), 103.

12. Berry, 104.

13. Graham Harman, *Bells and Whistles: More Speculative Realism* (Winchester: Zero Books, 2013), 6.

14. Bjarne Stroustrup in: Federico Biancuzzi and Shane Warden, eds., *Masterminds of Programming* (Sebastopol, CA: O'Reilly, 2009), 10.

15. Joe Armstrong, *Coders at Work: Reflections on the Craft of Programming*, ed. Peter Seibel (New York: Apress, 2009), 213.

16. A.I. Mikhailov, A.I. Chernyl, and R.S. Gilyarevskii, "Informatika – Novoe Nazvanie Teorii Naučnoj Informacii," *Naučno Tehničeskaja Informacija*, no. 12 (1966): 35–39.

17. Alessandro Bellini, "Is Metaphysics Relevant to Computer Science?," *Mathema* (blog), June 30, 2012, http://www.mathema.com/philosophy/metafisica/ is-metaphysics-relevant-to-computer-science/.

18. Miguel Penas López, "Speculative Experiments – What If Simondon and Harman Individuate Together?," in *Aesthetics in the 21st Century*, Speculations, V (New York: Punctum Books, 2014), 238.

19. Timothy Morton, "No It's Not Ethical Nihilism," Blog, *Ecology Without Nature* (blog), January 29, 2016, http://ecologywithoutnature.blogspot.com/2016/01/no-its-not-ethical-nihilism.html.

20. Graham Harman, *Tool-Being: Heidegger and the Metaphyics of Objects* (Chicago: Open Court, 2002), 262.

21. Markus Gabriel, *Why the World Does Not Exist* (Cambridge, UK: Polity Press, 2015).

22. Graham Harman, *Prince of Networks: Bruno Latour and Metaphysics*, Anamnesis (Melbourne: re.press, 2009), 186.

23. Quentin Meillassoux, *After Finitude: An Essay on the Necessity of Contingency* (London ; New York: Continuum, 2008), 5.

24. Colin McGinn, "Can We Solve the Mind-Body-Problem?," *Mind*, no. 98 (1989): 349–66; Godehard Brüntrup, "Mentale Verursachung und metaphysischer Realismus," *Theologie und Philosophie*, no. 70 (1995): 203–23.

25. Brüntrup, "Mentale Verursachung und metaphysischer Realismus," 222.

26. Meillassoux, *After Finitude*, 13.

27. Meillassoux, 5.

28. Ludwig Wittgenstein, *Tractatus logico-philosophicus*, ed. Joachim Schulte, 21. Aufl, vol. 1, Werkausgabe (Frankfurt am Main: Suhrkamp, 2014), 5.6.

29. Levi R. Bryant, *The Democracy of Objects*, 1. ed, New Metaphysics (Ann Arbor, Mich: Open Humanities Press, 2011), 37.

30. Gabriel, *Why the World Does Not Exist*, 8.

31. Gabriel, 50.

32. Bryant, *The Democracy of Objects*.

33. Meillassoux, *After Finitude*, 9.

34. Meillassoux, 11.

35. Graham Harman, "On the Undermining of Objects: Grant, Bruno, and Radical Philosophy," in *The Speculative Turn: Continental Materialism and Realism*, ed. Levi Bryant, Nick Srnicek, and Graham Harman (Melbourne: Re.Press, 2011), 21–40; Graham Harman, "Undermining, Overmining, and Duomining: A Critique," in *Add Metaphysics*, ed. Jane Bennett et al. (Aalto: Aalto Univ, 2013), 40–51.

36. Harman, *The Quadruple Object*, 6.

37. Harman, 11.

38. Harman, 12.

39. George Berkeley, *Principles of Human Knowledge and Three Dialogues*, ed. Howard Robinson (Oxford; New York: Oxford University Press, 1999), 25.

40. Graham Harman, "Space, Time, and Essence – An Object-Oriented Approach," in *Towards Speculative Realism: Essays and Lectures* (Winchester: Zero Books, 2010), 148.

41. Harman, *Prince of Networks*.

42. Bruno Latour, *Pasteur: guerre et paix des microbes*, Nouv. éd, La Découverte/poche Sciences humaines et sociales 114 (Paris: La Découverte, 2001).

43. Harman, *Prince of Networks*, 183.

44. Plato, *Plato's Meno*, trans. Dominic Scott, Cambridge Studies in the Dialogues of Plato (Cambridge, UK ; New York: Cambridge University Press, 2006).

45. Harman, *The Quadruple Object*, 67.

46. Harman, 67.

47. Harman, 67.

48. Saul A. Kripke, *Naming and Necessity* (Oxford: Blackwell, 1990), 19.

49. Harman, "Space, Time, and Essence – An Object-Oriented Approach," 147.

50. Harman, *The Quadruple Object*, 2011, 6.

51. Ian Bogost, "On Harman's 'The Quadruple Object'" (Lecture, June 23, 2012), http://www.youtube.com/watch?v=Bpmqg7OwgXg.

52. Kant, *CPR*, A38.

53. Harman, *The Quadruple Object*, 6.

54. Current research in physics, like the double-slit delayed choice quantum eraser experiment, suggests that time might actually be an effect of particle entanglement, but aiming to deduce metaphysical theories from observations in physical experiments would be far beyond the scope of this work. (Cord Friebe et al., *Philosophie der Quantenphysik: Einführung und Diskussion der zentralen Begriffe und Problemstellungen der Quantentheorie für Physiker und Philosophen*, Lehrbuch (Berlin: Springer, 2015).)

55. Harman, *The Quadruple Object*, 5.

56. Harman, 5.

57. Harman, "Space, Time, and Essence – An Object-Oriented Approach," 14.

58. Harman, *The Quadruple Object*, 6.

59. Harman, 116.

60. Gabriel, *Why the World Does Not Exist*, 64.

61. Harman, *The Quadruple Object*, 74.

62. Harman, 74.

63. Harman, 76.

64. Harman, 100.

65. Harman, "Space, Time, and Essence – An Object-Oriented Approach," 151.

66. Harman, 152.

67. Harman, 152.

68. Harman, *The Quadruple Object*, 98.

69. Harman, 100.

70. Martin Heidegger, *Sein und Zeit*, 19th ed. (Tübingen: Niemeyer, 2006), 71.

71. Harman, *Prince of Networks*, 185.

72. Harman, *The Quadruple Object*, 101.

73. Harman, 7.

74. Harman, *Prince of Networks*, 112.

75. Berry, *Critical Theory and the Digital*, 205.

76. Graham Harman, Personal communication, August 18, 2013.

77. Alan Shapiro, *Die Software der Zukunft oder: das Modell geht der Realität voraus*, International Flusser lectures (Köln: König, 2014), 7.

78. Gilbert Simondon, "The Genesis of the Individual," in *Incorporations*, ed. Jonathan Crary and Sanford Kwinter (New York: Zone, 1992), 301.

79. Bertrand Meyer, *Object-Oriented Software Construction*, Prentice-Hall International Series in Computer Science (New York: Prentice-Hall, 1988), 23.

80. These hierarchies should not be read as analogous to categories. A more fitting analogy would be ontological priority (objects further down in the hierarchy are contingent on those higher up).

81. Biancuzzi and Warden, *Masterminds of Programming*, 350.

82. Harman, *The Quadruple Object*, 69.

83. Vlad Tarko, "The Metaphysics of Object Oriented Programming," May 28, 2006, http://news.softpedia.com/news/The-Metaphysics-of-Object-Oriented-Programming-24906.shtml.

84. Anders Hejlsberg in: Biancuzzi and Warden, *Masterminds of Programming*, 315.

85. There is other terminology, but in this work we will use these classic terms in the sense defined in the C++ programming language

86. Microsoft, "CTime Class," 2015, https://msdn.microsoft.com/en-us/library/78zb0ese.aspx.

87. Simondon, "The Genesis of the Individual."

88. David R. Ditzel and David A. Patterson, "Retrospective on High-Level Language Computer Architecture" (ACM Press, 1980), 97–104, https://doi.org/10.1145/800053.801914.

89. A new generation of chips might end this separation. FPGAs are chips whose hardware can be modified by means of software, effectively blurring the line between software and hardware.

90. A. M. Turing, "On Computable Numbers, with an Application to the Entscheidungsproblem," *Proceedings of the London Mathematical Society* s2-42, no. 1 (January 1, 1937): 230–65, https://doi.org/10.1112/plms/s2-42.1.230; A. M. Turing, "On Computable Numbers, with an Application to the Entscheidungsproblem. A Correction," *Proceedings of the London Mathematical Society* s2-43, no. 6 (January 1, 1938): 544–46, https://doi.org/10.1112/plms/s2-43.6.544.

91. Graham Harman, "Art and Paradox" (Lecture, December 2011), 35:00, https://vimeo.com/53793807.

92. Harman, *The Quadruple Object*, 69.

93. Harman, 73.

94. The *singular they* is being used throughout this work as a gender-neutral pronoun in order to avoid the use of *he* where *she or he* actually is meant.

95. Benoît Mandelbrot, *Les objets fractals: forme, hasard et dimension*, 4th, rev. ed. ed., Champs 301 (Paris: Flammarion, 1995).

96. Harman, *The Quadruple Object*, 74.

97. Harman, 117.

98. Harman, 117.

99. Harman, 135.

100. Harman, 116.

101. Harman, 10.

102. cf. Graham Harman, *Immaterialism: Objects and Social Theory* (Malden, MA: Polity, 2016).

103. Jocelyn Benoist, "Realismus ohne Metaphysik," in *Der neue Realismus*, ed. Markus Gabriel, 2nd ed. (Berlin: Suhrkamp, 2015), 139.

104. Hans-Georg Gadamer, *Truth and Method*, ed. Joel Weinsheimer and Donald G. Marshall, 2nd, rev. ed. ed., Continuum Impacts (London: Continuum, 2004), 291.

105. Ibid., 294.

106. Gadamer, 295.

107. Gadamer, 236.

108. Gadamer, 294.

109. This includes artifacts of the absurd, as they are clearly identifiable as cultural artifacts.

110. Stefan Majetschak, *Ästhetik zur Einführung*, 4th, rev. ed. ed., Zur Einführung 334 (Hamburg: Junius, 2016), 113.

111. Harman only abandons the term intentional object in his own theory in favor of sensual object in *The Quadruple Object*.

112. Graham Harman, "Time, Space, Essence, and Eidos: A New Theory of Causation," ed. Arran Gare and Paul Ashton, *Cosmos and History: The Journal of Natural and Social Philosophy* 6, no. 1 (2010): 1–17.

113. Gadamer, Truth and Method, 292.

114. Plato, *Plato's Meno*, 80d1-4.

115. Gadamer, *Truth and Method*, 302.

116. Harold W. Noonan, *The Routledge Philosophy Guidebook to Kripke and Naming and Necessity*, Routledge Philosophy Guidebooks (New York: Routledge, 2013), 19.

117. Noonan, 6.

118. Kripke, *Naming and Necessity*, 91.

119. Noonan, *The Routledge Philosophy Guidebook to Kripke and Naming and Necessity*, 12.

120. Harman, *The Quadruple Object*, 74.

121. Graham Harman, *Guerrilla Metaphysics: Phenomenology and the Carpentry of Things* (Chicago: Open Court, 2005), 153.

122. Harman, 244.

123. Harman, *Prince of Networks*, 225.

124. Gadamer, *Truth and Method*, 295.

125. Harman, *The Quadruple Object*, 10.

126. Harman, 34.

127. Harman, 34.

128. Harman, 135.

129. see fig. 3.

130. Roy Bhaskar, *Critical Realism*, Faculti, 2014, www.youtube.com/watch?v=TO4FaaVy0Is.

131. Graham Harman, *Immaterialism: Objects and Social Theory* (Malden, MA: Polity, 2016).

132. Graham Harman, "On the Mesh, the Strange Stranger, and Hyperobjects: Morton's Ecological Ontology," *Tarp Architecture Manual*, no. Spring 2012 (2012): 16–19.

133. Timothy Morton, *Ecology without Nature: Rethinking Environmental Aesthetics*, 1. Harvard Univ. Press paperback ed (Cambridge, Mass.: Harvard Univ. Press, 2009).

134. We will eventually see that relatability is a necessary retroactive effect of the inter-fact (see chapter 5).

135. Harman, "Time, Space, Essence, and Eidos: A New Theory of Causation," 14.

136. Harman, *The Quadruple Object*, 95.

137. Harman, *Immaterialism*, 8.

138. Harman, *The Quadruple Object*, 35.

139. Harman however describes the rare case of direct contact between real and sensual objects, which he calls "sincerity," in which "the experiencer as a real object is in direct contact with a sensual object." (Harman, *The Quadruple Object*, 128) This is a somewhat mysterious position, as ooo actually holds that experiencing is not taking place unidirectionally, but is the sensual product of the confrontation of two real-object-poles.

140. Graham Harman, Personal communication, February 2016.

141. The Deleuzian differentiation of virtual and actual potentiality might come to mind: the repository of the real object is virtual in that it is both ideal and real, while the sensual object represents the actual and possible. Reading Harman through Deleuze, however, is beyond the scope of this work.

142. Muriel Combes, *Gilbert Simondon and the Philosophy of the Transindividual* (Cambridge, Mass.: MIT Press, 2013), 4.

143. Harman, "Time, Space, Essence, and Eidos: A New Theory of Causation," 14.

144. Harman leaves open the possibility for objects to have been united objects in the past but then to have ceased to exist as a united or joint object.

145. Objects in ooo are not identical to objects in set theory, and therefore Russell's paradox does not apply here.

146. Penas López, "Speculative Experiments – What If Simondon and Harman Individuate Together?," 235.

147. Tom Sparrow, *The End of Phenomenology: Metaphysics and the New Realism*, Speculative Realism (Edinburgh: Edinburgh University Press, 2014), 133.

148. Harman, *The Quadruple Object*, 122.

149. Harman, 122.

150. Harman, 121.

151. Harman, *Guerrilla Metaphysics*, 21.

152. Harman, *The Quadruple Object*, 134.

153. Harman, *The Quadruple Object*.

154. Timothy Morton, "The Mesh" (Lecture, May 22, 2009).

155. Graham Harman, "On the Mesh, the Strange Stranger, and Hyperobjects: Morton's Ecological Ontology," *Tarp Architecture Manual*, Spring 2012 (2012): 19.

156. Harman, 18.

157. Harman, "Time, Space, Essence, and Eidos: A New Theory of Causation," 14.

158. Harman, *The Quadruple Object*, 2011, 95.

159. Graham Harman, "The Road to Objects," *Continent.*, no. 1.3 (2011): 177.

160. Harman, *The Quadruple Object*, 143.

161. Harman, *Guerrilla Metaphysics*, 50.

162. Maurice Merleau-Ponty, *The Primacy of Perception: And Other Essays on Phenomenological Psychology, the Philosophy of Art, History and Politics*, ed. James M. Edie, 2nd ed., Northwestern University Studies in Phenomenology & Existential Philosophy (Evanston, Ill.: Northwestern Univ. Press, 1971), 16.

163. Graham Harman, Personal communication, December 13, 2013.

164. Harman, *The Quadruple Object*, 74.

165. Harman, *Tool-Being*, 262.

166. Graham Harman, "Ontography: The Rise of Objects," Blog, *Object-Oriented Philosophy* (blog), June 14, 2009, https://doctorzamalek2.wordpress.com/2009/07/14/ontography -the-rise-of-objects/.

167. Harman, *The Quadruple Object*, 143.

168. We will look into the additional dimensions of the object-pole diagrams in more detail in chapter 5.

169. Harman, "Time, Space, Essence, and Eidos: A New Theory of Causation," 1.

170. Harman, "Art and Paradox."

171. Simondon, "The Genesis of the Individual," 301.

172. Simondon, 318.

173. Simondon, 311.

174. Simondon, 311.

175. Simondon, 311.

176. Simondon, 318.

177. Simondon, 300.

178. Simondon, 311.

179. Georges Didi-Huberman, "Glimpses. Between Appearance and Disappearance," in *Schwerpunkt Verschwinden*, ed. Lorenz Engell and Bernhard Siegert, Zeitschrift für Medien- und Kulturforschung, 7/1/2016 (Hamburg: Felix Meiner Verlag, 2016), 109.

180. Paul Watzlawick, Janet Beavin Bavelas, and Don D. Jackson, *Pragmatics of Human Communication: A Study of Interactional Patterns, Pathologies, and Paradoxes* (New York: Norton, 1967), 51.

181. Graham Harman, "Undermining, Overmining, and Duomining: A Critique," in *Add Metaphysics*, ed. Jane Bennett et al., Crossover. Aalto University Publication Series C, 1/2013 (Aalto: Aalto Univ, 2013), 40–51.

182. Harman, *Immaterialism*.

183. Harman, "On the Mesh, the Strange Stranger, and Hyperobjects: Morton's Ecological Ontology," 19.

184. Simondon, "The Genesis of the Individual," 298.

185. Harman, *Immaterialism*, 18.

186. Harman, 32.

187. Simondon, "The Genesis of the Individual," 307.

188. Harman, *Immaterialism*, 18.

189. These new objects are generated from a relation of real-object-poles and sensual-object-poles. However, discussing the consequences of this possibility would be beyond the scope of the present work.

190. Harman, "Time, Space, Essence, and Eidos: A New Theory of Causation," 16.

191. Simondon, "The Genesis of the Individual," 297.

192. Sergei Eisenstein, *Film Form: Essays in Film Theory*, trans. Jay Leyda, A Harvest Book 153 (New York: Harcourt, Brace & World, 1977), 45.

193. Armen Avanessian and Anke Hennig, *Metanoia: spekulative Ontologie der Sprache*, Orig.-Ausg, Internationaler Merve-Diskurs 407 (Berlin: Merve, 2014).

194. Stanley Kubrick, *2001: A Space Odyssey* (Metro-Goldwyn-Mayer, 1968).

195. Simondon, "The Genesis of the Individual," 318.

196. Harman, *The Quadruple Object*, 126.

197. Gadamer, *Truth and Method*, 295.

198. Gadamer, 291.

199. Simondon, "The Genesis of the Individual," 299.

200. Simondon, 311.

201. Simondon, 301.

202. Harman, *The Quadruple Object*, 100.

203. Simondon, "The Genesis of the Individual," 298.

204. Simondon, 318.

205. Penas López, "Speculative Experiments – What If Simondon and Harman Individuate Together?"

206. Penas López, 242.

207. Penas López, 239.

208. Penas López, 245.

209. Penas López, 235.

210. Harman, "The Road to Objects," 172.

211. Harman, *Immaterialism*, 6.

212. Penas López, "Speculative Experiments – What If Simondon and Harman Individuate Together?," 237.

213. Harman, "Time, Space, Essence, and Eidos: A New Theory of Causation," 14.

214. Simondon, "The Genesis of the Individual," 298.

215. Penas López, "Speculative Experiments – What If Simondon and Harman Individuate Together?," 237.

216. Penas López, 237.

217. Simondon, "The Genesis of the Individual," 300.

218. Harman, Guerrilla *Metaphysics*, 244.

219. Harman, Personal communication.

220. Harman, The *Quadruple Object*, 174.

221. To give just one example, in a world in which the sensual and real are one, every reality is always already fully realized. There could be no emergence, as no object would hold any surplus.

222. Franz Brentano, *Psychologie vom empirischen Standpunkte*, ed. Thomas Binder and Arkadiusz Chrudzimski, Sämtliche veröffentlichte Schriften Schriften zur Psychologie, Franz Brentano. Hrsg. von Thomas Binder...; Abt. 1[...] ; Bd. 1 (Heusenstamm: Ontos, 2008), 124.

223. Harman, *The Quadruple Object*, 20.

224. Harman, Personal communication.

225. Harman, *Guerrilla Metaphysics*, 26.

226. Harman, 26.

227. Harman, 26.

228. Harman, Personal communication.

229. Meillassoux, *After Finitude*, 3.

230. Peter Oberhofer, "Quentin Meillassoux: Nach der Endlichkeit. Versuch über die Notwendigkeit der Kontingenz," Journal Phänomenologie, no. 31 (2009): 88.

231. Meillassoux, *After Finitude*, 30.

232. Meillassoux, 105.

233. René Descartes, *Discours de La Méthode* (Primento Digital Publishing, 2015), http://public.eblib.com/choice/publicfullrecord.aspx?p=4093644.

234. Meillassoux, *After Finitude*, 3.

235. Meillassoux, 3.

236. Meillassoux, 126.

237. Meillassoux, 126.

238. Meillassoux, 12.

239. Meillassoux, 115.

240. Harman, *Immaterialism*, 12.

241. Harman, 12.

242. Meillassoux, *After Finitude*, 3.

243. Federico Biancuzzi in: Biancuzzi and Warden, *Masterminds of Programming*, x.

244. Harman, *Guerrilla Metaphysics*, 21.

245. Harman, 22.

246. Harman, "Time, Space, Essence, and Eidos: A New Theory of Causation," 14.

247. Graham Harman, "Black Holes" (Lecture, August 19, 2014), https://www.youtube.com/watch?v=p1_R-Zbv5G4.

248. Harman, *The Quadruple Object*, 100.

249. Penas López, "Speculative Experiments – What If Simondon and Harman Individuate Together?," 239.

250. Penas López, 243.

251. Lambert Wiesing, *Das Mich der Wahrnehmung: eine Autopsie*, Suhrkamp Taschenbuch Wissenschaft 2171 (Frankfurt am Main: Suhrkamp, 2015).

252. Simondon, "The Genesis of the Individual," 305.

253. Simondon, 318.

254. Simondon, 318.

255. Simondon, 301.

256. Simondon, 306.

257. Harman, *The Quadruple Object*, 69.

258. Penas López, "Speculative Experiments – What If Simondon and Harman Individuate Together?," 239.

259. Harman, *Immaterialism*, 17.

260. Harman, "Time, Space, Essence, and Eidos: A New Theory of Causation," 14.

261. Penas López, "Speculative Experiments – What If Simondon and Harman Individuate Together?," 239.

262. Harman, "Time, Space, Essence, and Eidos: A New Theory of Causation," 17.

263. Harman, 1.

264. Harman, *The Quadruple Object*, 102.

265. Harman, Personal communication.

266. Simondon, "The Genesis of the Individual," 300.

Bibliography

Armstrong, Joe. *Coders at Work: Reflections on the Craft of Programming*. Edited by Peter Seibel. New York: Apress, 2009.

Avanessian, Armen, and Anke Hennig. *Metanoia: spekulative Ontologie der Sprache*. Orig.-Ausg. Internationaler Merve-Diskurs 407. Berlin: Merve, 2014.

Bellini, Alessandro. "Is Metaphysics Relevant to Computer Science?" *Mathema* (blog), June 30, 2012. http://www.mathema.com/philosophy/metafisica/is-metaphysics-relevant-to-computer-science/.

Benoist, Jocelyn. "Realismus ohne Metaphysik." In *Der neue Realismus*, edited by Markus Gabriel, 2nd ed. Berlin: Suhrkamp, 2015.

Berkeley, George. *Principles of Human Knowledge and Three Dialogues*. Edited by Howard Robinson. Oxford; New York: Oxford University Press, 1999.

Berry, David M. *Critical Theory and the Digital*. Critical Theory and Contemporary Society. New York: Bloomsbury, 2014.

Bhaskar, Roy. *Critical Realism*. Faculti, 2014. www.youtube.com/watch?v=TO4FaaVy0Is.

Biancuzzi, Federico, and Shane Warden, eds. *Masterminds of Programming*. Sebastopol, CA: O'Reilly, 2009.

Bogost, Ian. *Alien Phenomenology, or, What It's like to Be a Thing*. Posthumanities 20. Minneapolis: University of Minnesota Press, 2012.

————. "On Harman's 'The Quadruple Object.'" Lecture presented at the Presentation of MétaphysiqueS book series, net.culture club MaMa, Zagreb, June 23, 2012. http://www.youtube.com/watch?v=Bpmqg7OwgXg.

Brentano, Franz. *Psychologie vom empirischen Standpunkte.* Edited by Thomas Binder and Arkadiusz Chrudzimski. Sämtliche veröffentlichte Schriften Schriften zur Psychologie, Franz Brentano. Hrsg. von Thomas Binder...; Abt. 1[...] ; Bd. 1. Heusenstamm: Ontos, 2008.

Brüntrup, Godehard. "Mentale Verursachung und metaphysischer Realismus." *Theologie und Philosophie*, no. 70 (1995): 203–23.

Bryant, Levi R. *The Democracy of Objects.* 1. ed. New Metaphysics. Ann Arbor, Mich: Open Humanities Press, 2011.

Combes, Muriel. *Gilbert Simondon and the Philosophy of the Transindividual.* Cambridge, Mass.: MIT Press, 2013.

Descartes, René. *Discours de La Méthode.* Primento Digital Publishing, 2015. http://public.eblib.com/choice/publicfullrecord.aspx?p=4093644.

Didi-Huberman, Georges. "Glimpses. Between Appearance and Disappearance." In *Schwerpunkt Verschwinden*, edited by Lorenz Engell and Bernhard Siegert, 109–24. Zeitschrift für Medien- und Kulturforschung, 7/1/2016. Hamburg: Felix Meiner Verlag, 2016.

Ditzel, David R., and David A. Patterson. "Retrospective on High-Level Language Computer Architecture," 97–104. ACM Press, 1980. https://doi.org/10.1145/800053.801914.

Eco, Umberto. *Opera aperta: forma e indeterminazione nelle poetiche contemporanee.* Milan: Bompiani, 2013.

Eisenstein, Sergei. *Film Form: Essays in Film Theory.* Translated by Jay Leyda. A Harvest Book 153. New York: Harcourt, Brace & World, 1977.

Friebe, Cord, Meinhard Kuhlmann, Holger Lyre, Paul Näger, Oliver Passon, and Manfred Stöckler. *Philosophie der Quantenphysik: Einführung und Diskussion der zentralen Begriffe und Problemstellungen der Quantentheorie für Physiker und Philosophen.* Lehrbuch. Berlin: Springer, 2015.

Gabriel, Markus. *Why the World Does Not Exist.* Cambridge, UK: Polity Press, 2015.

Gadamer, Hans-Georg. *Truth and Method.* Edited by Joel Weinsheimer and Donald G. Marshall. 2nd, rev. ed. ed. Continuum Impacts. London: Continuum, 2004.

Harman, Graham. "Art and Paradox." Lecture presented at the The Matter of Contradiction/Ungrounding the Object, Paris, France, December 2011. https://vimeo.com/53793807.

———. *Bells and Whistles: More Speculative Realism.* Winchester: Zero Books, 2013.

———. "Black Holes." Lecture presented at the European Graduate School Public Lectures, Saas-Fee, Switzerland, August 19, 2014. https://www.youtube.com/watch?v=p1_R-Zbv5G4.

———. *Guerrilla Metaphysics: Phenomenology and the Carpentry of Things.* Chicago: Open Court, 2005.

———. *Immaterialism: Objects and Social Theory.* Malden, MA: Polity, 2016.

———. "On the Mesh, the Strange Stranger, and Hyperobjects: Morton's Ecological Ontology." *Tarp Architecture Manual,* no. Spring 2012 (2012): 16–19.

———. "On the Undermining of Objects: Grant, Bruno, and Radical Philosophy." In *The Speculative Turn: Continental Materialism and Realism,* edited by Levi Bryant, Nick Srnicek, and Graham Harman, 21–40. Melbourne: Re.Press, 2011.

———. "Ontography: The Rise of Objects." Blog. *Object-Oriented Philosophy* (blog), June 14, 2009. https://doctorzamalek2.wordpress.com/2009/07/14/ontography-the-rise-of-objects/.

———. *Prince of Networks: Bruno Latour and Metaphysics.* Anamnesis. Melbourne: re.press, 2009.

———. "Space, Time, and Essence – An Object-Oriented Approach." In *Towards Speculative Realism: Essays and Lectures,* 140–69. Winchester: Zero Books, 2010.

———. *The Quadruple Object.* Winchester, U.K.: Zero Books, 2011.

———. "The Road to Objects." *Continent.*, no. 1.3 (2011): 171–79.

———. "Time, Space, Essence, and Eidos: A New Theory of Causation." Edited by Arran Gare and Paul Ashton. *Cosmos and History: The Journal of Natural and Social Philosophy* 6, no. 1 (2010): 1–17.

———. *Tool-Being: Heidegger and the Metaphyics of Objects.* Chicago: Open Court, 2002.

———. "Undermining, Overmining, and Duomining: A Critique." In *Add Metaphysics*, edited by Jane Bennett, Vera Bühlmann, Graham Harman, Ines Weizman, Andrew Witt, and Jenna Sutela, 40–51. Crossover. Aalto University Publication Series C, 1/2013. Aalto: Aalto Univ, 2013.

Heidegger, Martin. *Sein und Zeit.* 19th ed. Tübingen: Niemeyer, 2006.

Kant, Immanuel. *Critique of Pure Reason.* Edited by Paul Guyer and Allen W. Wood. The Cambridge Edition of the Works of Immanuel Kant. Cambridge: Cambridge University Press, 1998.

Kripke, Saul A. *Naming and Necessity.* Oxford: Blackwell, 1990.

Kubrick, Stanley. *2001: A Space Odyssey.* Metro-Goldwyn-Mayer, 1968.

Latour, Bruno. *Pasteur: guerre et paix des microbes.* Nouv. éd. La Découverte/poche Sciences humaines et sociales 114. Paris: La Découverte, 2001.

Majetschak, Stefan. *Ästhetik zur Einführung.* 4th, rev. ed. ed. Zur Einführung 334. Hamburg: Junius, 2016.

Mandelbrot, Benoît. *Les objets fractals: forme, hasard et dimension.* 4th, rev. ed. ed. Champs 301. Paris: Flammarion, 1995.

McGinn, Colin. "Can We Solve the Mind-Body-Problem?" *Mind*, no. 98 (1989): 349–66.

Meillassoux, Quentin. *After Finitude: An Essay on the Necessity of Contingency.* London ; New York: Continuum, 2008.

Merleau-Ponty, Maurice. *The Primacy of Perception: And Other Essays on Phenomenological Psychology, the Philosophy of Art, History and Politics.* Edited by

James M. Edie. 2nd ed. Northwestern University Studies in Phenomenology & Existential Philosophy. Evanston, Ill.: Northwestern Univ. Press, 1971.

Meyer, Bertrand. *Object-Oriented Software Construction*. Prentice-Hall International Series in Computer Science. New York: Prentice-Hall, 1988.

Microsoft. "CTime Class," 2015. https://msdn.microsoft.com/en-us/library/78zb0ese.aspx.

Mikhailov, A.I., A.I. Chernyl, and R.S. Gilyarevskii. "Informatika – Novoe Nazvanie Teorii Naučnoj Informacii." Naučno Tehničeskaja *Informacija*, no. 12 (1966): 35–39.

Morton, Timothy. *Ecology without Nature: Rethinking Environmental Aesthetics*. 1. Harvard Univ. Press paperback ed. Cambridge, Mass.: Harvard Univ. Press, 2009.

———. "No It's Not Ethical Nihilism." Blog. *Ecology Without Nature* (blog), January 29, 2016. http://ecologywithoutnature.blogspot.com/2016/01/no-its-not-ethical-nihilism.html.

———. "The Mesh." Lecture presented at the Beyond Environmentalism: Culture, Justice, and Global Ecologies, Santa Barbara, CA, May 22, 2009.

Noonan, Harold W. *The Routledge Philosophy Guidebook to Kripke and Naming and Necessity*. Routledge Philosophy Guidebooks. New York: Routledge, 2013.

Oberhofer, Peter. "Quentin Meillassoux: Nach Der Endlichkeit. Versuch Über Die Notwendigkeit Der Kontingenz." *Journal Phänomenologie*, no. 31 (2009): 86–89.

Penas López, Miguel. "Speculative Experiments – What If Simondon and Harman Individuate Together?" In *Aesthetics in the 21st Century*, 225–50. Speculations, V. New York: Punctum Books, 2014.

Plato. *Plato's Meno*. Translated by Dominic Scott. Cambridge Studies in the Dialogues of Plato. Cambridge, UK ; New York: Cambridge University Press, 2006.

Shapiro, Alan. *Die Software der Zukunft oder: das Modell geht der Realität voraus*. International Flusser lectures. Köln: König, 2014.

Simondon, Gilbert. "The Genesis of the Individual." In *Incorpora-tions*, edited by Jonathan Crary and Sanford Kwinter, 297–319. New York: Zone, 1992.

Sparrow, Tom. *The End of Phenomenology: Metaphysics and the New Realism.* Speculative Realism. Edinburgh: Edinburgh University Press, 2014.

Tarko, Vlad. "The Metaphysics of Object Oriented Programming," May 28, 2006. http://news.softpedia.com/news/The-Metaphysics-of-Object-Orient-ed-Programming-24906.shtml.

Turing, A. M. "On Computable Numbers, with an Application to the Ents-cheidungsproblem." *Proceedings of the London Mathematical Society* s2-42, no. 1 (January 1, 1937): 230–65. https://doi.org/10.1112/plms/s2-42.1.230.

———. "On Computable Numbers, with an Application to the Entscheid-ungsproblem. A Correction." *Proceedings of the London Mathematical Soci-ety* s2-43, no. 6 (January 1, 1938): 544–46. https://doi.org/10.1112/plms/s2-43.6.544.

Watzlawick, Paul, Janet Beavin Bavelas, and Don D. Jackson. *Pragmatics of Human Communication: A Study of Interactional Patterns, Pathologies, and Paradoxes.* New York: Norton, 1967.

Wiesing, Lambert. *Das Mich der Wahrnehmung: eine Autopsie.* Suhrkamp Taschenbuch Wissenschaft 2171. Frankfurt am Main: Suhrkamp, 2015.

Wittgenstein, Ludwig. *Tractatus logico-philosophicus.* Edited by Joachim Schulte. 21. Aufl. Vol. 1. 8 vols. Werkausgabe. Frankfurt am Main: Suhrkamp, 2014.

www.ingramcontent.com/pod-product-compliance
Lightning Source LLC
Chambersburg PA
CBHW071139050326
40690CB00008B/1508